DATE DUE

	PRINTED IN U.S.A.

The Drugstore Liberal

by Robert Sherrill

THE DRUGSTORE LIBERAL
GOTHIC POLITICS IN THE DEEP SOUTH
THE ACCIDENTAL PRESIDENT

Robert Sherrill and Harry W. Ernst

THE DRUGSTORE LIBERAL

Grossman Publishers   New York   1968

*For Izzy Stone
and Peter*

"I fancy a number of people all over the western world still think of themselves as liberals, but are in essence no such thing. In their hearts they believe that their society won't (and shouldn't) change much, that communism is the enemy absolute and that the only tasks open to men of good will are to fight the Cold War with one hand and perform minor benevolent activities with the other. This is a tenable attitude, but it is one of people who have given up the intellectual struggle."

— Sir Charles P. Snow

No! I am not Prince Hamlet, nor was meant to be;
Am an attendant lord, one that will do
To swell a progress, start a scene or two,
Advise the prince; no doubt, an easy tool,
Deferential, glad to be of use,
Politic, cautious, and meticulous;
Full of high sentence, but a bit obtuse;
At times, indeed, almost ridiculous—
Almost, at times, the Fool.

The Love Song of J. Alfred Prufrock,
— T. S. Eliot

Contents

Speaking in Tongues, or, The Art of Being Hubert Humphrey

On May 22, 1965, at the very hour that President Johnson was meeting with military advisers in the White House to discuss the merits of blockading the coast of South Vietnam, Hubert Humphrey was in New York City being inducted as a full-scale bona fide member of the Girl Scouts, at the conclusion of which ceremony he rubbed his hands together and exclaimed, "Well, gee! I'm just delighted. Just wait until I get back to Washington and tell the President about this!"

To many liberals who would like to think that Humphrey is a different kind of political creature from Lyndon Baines Johnson, the booted and spurred wheeler-dealer, episodes such as this are treasured like pressed flower petals between the pages of their Book of the Hours. *This*, they say, is the great old Hubert they once knew and relied on. A changed man now, they lament, "a hatchetman," as *The Progressive* magazine put it; "the betrayer of the liberal movement," in the indignant words of Alfred Kazin and Irving Howe. But wiser men, or wilier men, know better. "What nonsense it is," said former UN Ambassador Arthur Goldberg, "to suggest that my old friend Hubert Humphrey has changed."

He has not changed at all; the appearance of change comes from the fact that, as the most phenomenal rotor rooter of contemporary politics, new substances are now being brought to the surface. He is deceptively plain.

He lives in his own elm-lined, homogenized world. His idea of attaining dignity was illustrated a month after he became vice president when he gave a fraternity house the nickel-plated nickelodeon that had been part of his household furniture. His mastery of that most typically American humor, the self-depreciating wisecrack (Friend: "Hey, Hubert, you're becoming a myth!" Humphrey: "Yeah, a myth-fit") has increased under the adversity of office. "Daniel Webster [he likes to say] refused this high honor, saying 'I do not propose to be buried until I'm really dead and in a coffin.' But not Hubert Humphrey." He has always been a jolly, decent sort of fellow; he has always stood for a reasonably fixed code of fair play (athough he has broken that code at several important junctions in his life, for which he was received widely as a "practical" politician). It pains him to see anybody who is hungry or homeless, and he hopes someday that the government can do something to relieve their destitution, after it has first beaten back Communism around the world. He laments the fact that Negroes are killed or otherwise mistreated, but he thinks the government has gone about as far as it should go in legislating civil rights. He believes that sanity lies in disarmament, but only from a "position of strength." In short, Hubert Humphrey is a good American.

In some of his responses to life, he is soft and pliable almost to the point of womanliness, and some of his remarks seem to indicate that he sees himself in this way. "I'm Lyndon Johnson's Eleanor Roosevelt," he once said to delegates of an American Newspaper Guild convention. "She used to get out and see and tell her great husband what was going on in the country. That's what I do for the president." On several other occasions he has likened the president-vice president relationship to a "marriage with no divorce" and himself to the "wife." During the period when Johnson was going through the rigamarole of "looking" for a running mate in 1964, he frequently consulted with Humphrey, who recalls it in these romantic terms: "He discussed every move and thought with me as if nothing could interest me less personally. It's like a guy calling the girl next door—who he knows is madly in love with him—to ask the phone number of the newest broad in town." His distaste for the Kennedys, usually worded along class lines, includes this plain girl view of himself. "The whole Kennedy family," he said in 1964, "has talent *in depth*. No newspaper publishers knew *my* father. Sargent Shriver was head of Merchandise Mart; I was head of Humphrey's Drug Store . . . and what's glamorous about the name Humphrey? I'm not glamorous *per se*. I'm not young, I'm not old, I'm like the girl next door—always available but you don't necessarily think about marriage."

Johnson once said of Humphrey that "he gets a lot of emotion into his work . . . Hubert can cry pretty good over something." Indeed he can. He weeps easily. His close friends who would prefer that he not be under the domination of Lyndon Johnson insist that he cries more commonly these days than ever, one friend explaining "he's being torn apart." But tears have always been readily available, for both unimportant and tragic occasions, and for little disappointments and peeves. He wept in 1956 when he was bypassed for the vice-presidential nomination by the Democratic national convention. He wept in his Charleston hotel room and again at his campaign headquarters on the night in 1960 that it was clear John Kennedy had just drubbed him in the West Virginia primary. On a recent tour of Asia, he became so emotionally overwrought while touring a hospital where GI's from Vietnam were being treated that the entourage of reporters was asked not to follow him. Shortly after returning from a tour of Europe, he spoke to a group of Jewish women in Atlanta, Georgia, and in the midst of his speech he announced that "my heart is just broken because the press shows Europe the wrong side of this country," and he began to weep. Tears come just as fast, however, for no reason other than that the day has been exhausting. It is not rare for him to end a difficult newspaper interview with sobs.

While this softer side of Humphrey appeals to many people, it irritates others because it contrasts sharply with certain policies he supports, such as the war in Vietnam, and Alfred Kazin very likely had the tearful Humphrey in mind when he angrily accused him of engaging in militant behavior "to prove your masculinity."

The weeping hawk also offends old friends such as Murray Kempton, to whom Humphrey is not only now beyond mercy but also beneath contempt as an antagonist:

"It is cruel and inhuman to picket Hubert Humphrey, to get up and leave the room when he rises to speak, to slip, as two young people did, into a hotel to cry 'murderer' at him. It is even cruel and inhuman to comment upon him with polite detachment. For the Vice President of the United States bleeds from the smallest pebble shied his way by the feeblest wrist. An admonitory pat can break a bone."

While it is easy to feel disgust for Humphrey, it is difficult to be angry with him. After a political party meeting in Minneapolis, at which Humphrey presided, Ben DuBois, who used to be national secretary of the Independent Bankers Association, went to Humphrey and said, "You conducted yourself very undemocratically and terribly at this meeting. Furthermore, Hubert, you talk too goddamn much." Hubert shook his hand, gripped him on the shoulder and said, "Ben, you're absolutely right." Humphrey's long-time political foe, former Minnesota Governor Elmer Benson, said he once criticized Humphrey harshly in public "and after the meeting he came over and shook hands with me and said, 'Elmer, I want to thank you very much for calling my attention to it.' That's his style—the guy is fantastic. How can you argue with a man who agrees with you?"

In 1929, just before the crash, Humphrey's father took him from their home in Doland, South Dakota, to the University of Minnesota for his first abortive try at a college education, and let him out of the Model A with the advice: "Good-bye. Good luck. Grow up." In a sometimes appealing way, Humphrey never did. He is still the friendly fat kid on the block. The time-honored test of politicians, brought to a climax in the career of Richard Nixon ("Would you buy a used car from this man?") is passed easily by Humphrey. And if the next morning your HHH Used Car refused to start, Hubert would cheerfully drive across town to give you a shove, and he would do it in such a swell style that instead of fussing about being cheated you would go away saying nice things about the neighborliness of that pudgy huckster.

When he first came to Washington he was described by one writer as "too cocky, too slick, too shallow, too ambitious, a brain-picker rather than a scholar, clever without being wise." He improved with age; he is no longer too cocky or too slick. He is more of a brain-picker than ever, but what politician in Washington isn't? As for his shallowness, this is a treacherous measure of any man, and especially is it a treacherous measure of Humphrey. He *is* shallow, in that he spreads himself too thin, over too many topics. But all these thin layers are laminated into a rather imposing depth. In a typical week during his Senate career, Humphrey took the floor to discuss—among many other topics—the migratory-bird–hunting stamp, the Armed-Forces chess tourney, dairy reports, disaster loans, disarmament, domestic economy, price supports, consumer problems, trade development, antitrust laws, the public debt, the North African policy, the trickery of Richard Nixon, the stupidity of Harold Stassen, passports, French politics, international civil aviation, Lithuanian independence, captive nations, the wildflowers of the Northwest, and the need for more office space. He can talk with journeyman information on just about any topic of importance now before Washington, and this has been true during most of the past two decades. His memory does it. It is a vacuum file cabinet. When he was in pharmacy school, before going to work in his dad's drugstore during the Depression, he learned by heart all the drugs, all their Latin names, all the prescribed dosages, listed in the druggists' *Pharmacopaeia*. It was a feat comparable to memorizing all the words and definitions in an abridged dictionary.

Twenty years ago one of his aides was also quoted as saying of him, "The trouble with Humphrey is he never takes time out. He's never alone with himself. If the guy would only sit down with himself and say, 'What am I all about?' But he's afraid to ask himself that question." He still is.

Not even all men who know Humphrey well can agree on his depth or on his endurance. Even from those who praise him for his broad grasp of topics one often detects a questioning note. Senator William Fulbright of Arkansas, who sat with Humphrey for years on the Foreign Relations Committee and was in his social group, draws back cautiously a moment after beginning his praise: "Hubert could talk on any subject at any length. He had sympathy for *Every*body. He was interested in *Every*thing—and everything equally. He was fun to have around. He was friendly as a pup. Everybody in the Senate tried to accommodate him—if it was convenient. [Here Fulbright paused reflectively.] I don't remember his being terribly effective. I don't remember his name being associated with anything much, unless perhaps it was civil rights. [How about disarmament?] Oh, he was interested in that for a while, but then he seemed to drop it."

The seas of his senatorial rhetoric were often so choppy that it was hard to take a sounding. Emphasizing evangelism over logic, his speeches in the Senate (since ascending to the vice presidency his speech-writers have usually forced him to restrain himself from neofundamentalisms) were regularly larded with references to the "spirit of the Lord" and "a heavenly reward" and scriptural quotes. Not for him are the agricultural intellectualisms of a Henry Wallace. "The ever-normal granary" and such concepts are for hayseed philosophers, not for Humphrey; he copes with food and farm problems, as he does with most problems, on a tearful, emotional level. The foreign-aid–supported wheat program he

has touted since coming to Washington has meant millions
of dollars in profits to his region, but he has seldom talked
about it in those terms. Usually, in his holiness style, he has
approached it as a chance for a greedy America to repent of its
sins and feed the starvin' heathen. "I say we are immoral!"
(This is from one of his early speeches, January 5, 1950, but
the tone was constant throughout most of his Senate career.)
"We are almost anti-Christian! We ought to get down on our
knees and pray to God to forgive us for our sins, for here
on the Eastern coast of our land are Liberty ships, 10,000-ton
freighters, loaded with wheat which the Commodity Credit
Corporation has purchased, and the wheat is rotting. The
wheat is stored up, and here are people in India dying of
hunger, with the Communists on top of them, with their
government almost tottering. And what are we doing? . . ."
etc. Later he admitted he might have been wrong about the
wheat rotting—but he felt that that was a liberty not to be
held against a good sermon—and he did not retract his judgment of our sins, as in fact he was right in not doing. The appeals to send U.S. farm surpluses to India and Pakistan were
the first step toward the Food-for-Peace program, which today
accounts for half of all non-military foreign aid.

And yet, here again, there is no stability to Humphrey's
view. Often stressing that hunger breeds communism, he will
nevertheless agree with people who hold just the opposite.
On June 6, 1956, he was touting in the Senate an article coauthored by Walter Rostow (then with MIT, now chief hawk
in Lyndon Johnson's birdhouse) which took the position that
it is a "serious misconception" that "revolt and protest are
the result of hunger and poverty and that relieving hunger
and reducing poverty will therefore reduce revolutionary
pressure."

On the point of his changeability, no one can speak with
more knowledge (and with more tolerance) than Senator Joseph
Clark of Pennsylvania, the charming, urbane cynic who looked
upon Humphrey as "a kind of father confessor" from the day
Clark entered the Senate in 1957 until Humphrey left in

1964. Sometimes it seems that just about every other politician in Washington likes ol' Hubert, but few of them are his intimate friends; Clark is among the few. Thinking back to their days together in the Senate, Clark has had this to say: "Hubert was very good, you know—and I say this not in a critical sense—Hubert's been very good about riding two or three horses at once. He was able to keep his ins with Lyndon and even some Southerners without, to my way of thinking, sacrificing his inherent liberalism or infringing in any way on my loyalty to him. Paul [Douglas] was a little suspicious of Hubert—Paul's a real Calvinist, and he felt—I didn't—that Hubert was trying too much to be all things to all people. Hubert was the leader [of the liberal coterie]. He was the guy we had to look to. He was the Whip. Sure, he was riding two or three horses, but we knew it. I realize that it's easy enough to take Hubert apart, but when you compare him to the present Whip he looks pretty good. Now, because he touched bases in a lot of places where the rest of us couldn't touch base, I think he had a pretty realistic appraisal of the art of the possible."

Clark recalled that a month or two before the Democratic convention in 1964 he had a "long heart-to-heart talk with him. We were riding down from the Capitol to the White House in a taxicab, and I let him have it good and hard. I said, 'I just don't think you ought to do it. You'll get yourself in a bind where you can't be yourself. Your future is in the Senate, and from the Senate possibly to the presidency. God knows you know how I love you, but I think if you take the vice presidency you're just going to become a prisoner.' And he said, 'Joe, I don't care anything about being vice president.' I believed him at the time, but of course it wasn't true. He was dying to get it." (How gullible can friends be? Everyone in Washington—except Clark, apparently—knew he was sweating to get the nomination.)

When asked if he thought the things Humphrey was saying as vice president reflect his inner feelings, Clark responded:

"No. Maybe he's kidding himself. He has a pretty good capacity for self-delusion, self-deception. We all do. Hubert more than most."

Why would Humphrey tell him, a close friend, that he had no desire for the vice presidency when he obviously did covet it?

"When he was talking to me he didn't want it. When he was talking to Lyndon, he sure as hell did. Kinda like a chameleon—sometimes green, sometimes brown."

Isn't that a disastrous thing to say about a friend?

"Depends on whether you're a Calvinist or not," said Clark, smiling. "I don't know—guess I'm a little more tolerant. I'd even kid him about it. He'd just laugh. And say, 'Oh, Joe.' "

The Senate is an "oh Joe" place. But outside the Senate many—accustomed to a different ethic and a different criterion for what is possible and perhaps even accustomed to different synonyms for friendly chameleons—are more critical of Humphrey.

Once Humphrey went on a hedgehopping air trip with A. M. Keith, a Minnesota politician, and wherever they stopped a local dignitary would come aboard and Humphrey would welcome him and ask about his family. At some point in the conversation Humphrey would ask him what church he belonged to. If he said, "I'm a Methodist," Humphrey would smile joyfully and say, "I'm a Methodist, too." If at the next stop the reply was "Episcopalian," then Humphrey (who is a Congregationalist) would respond, "Well, that's what I am. Glad to meet another!" He told Baptists he was a Baptist, Lutherans he was a Lutheran, etc. Keith finally took Humphrey aside and said, "Gosh, Hubert, you're going to get caught up on this. You can't tell everybody you belong to their church." Humphrey seemed to be actually puzzled. "Why not?" he asked, "I'm a Christian."

He has spent his mature life proving that he believes that the faith of a politician, like that of a Christian, covers almost all splinter concepts. He spreads himself so thin, over so many issues, and wobbles in so many directions, that he has been called an opportunist by some, for which he has, as always, a fast answer: "What's wrong with taking advantage of the opportunities?"

Humphrey's sail has always been set to catch the slightest change in the wind. At the 1944 Democratic national convention he was a rabid advocate of Henry Wallace as vice-presidential candidate. The *Washington Post* gave this picture: "Few who watched the Democratic convention closely will ever forget the sight of Humphrey and Barney Allen, a Red River Valley farmer, their clothes half torn off their backs and their voices gone, racing through the Chicago stadium carrying an American flag and a Wallace banner, begging and pleading with the delegates to support their man." Wallace's outlook changed very little in the next few years, but the policy of the United States became much sterner toward Communism, and therefore by 1946 it was prudent for a politically ambitious young man, which Humphrey certainly was, to shed some of his old friendships and alliances. Humphrey dumped Wallace, calling him "totally irresponsible," and by 1948 he was denouncing him as a fellow traveler.

Those who admire Humphrey as an opportunist will often praise him in disastrously friendly ways, as did columnist George Sokolsky in 1956 when he wrote, to defend Humphrey against the "radical" designation, "He is an educated man who apparently finds it possible to compromise with his knowledge and training for political advantage."

He will talk for just about any group on just about any topic, and most of his speeches support the description Lyndon Johnson gave of Humphrey as "a man who prepares for a solid, thought-provoking speech by taking a deep breath." His windiness has created an encyclopedia of apocryphal tales very easy to believe; like the time a group of volunteer advisers met with him, only to be drowned in a ninety-minute monologue, so they picked up their hats, said it was obvious he didn't think he needed any advice, and quit. He has an endless catalog of shibboleths and personal clichés, and his comments on any of the code topics are totally predictable. If he is to address a farm group, for example, he will inevitably tell about how he and his father used to vaccinate hogs during the Depression. But questions relating to immediate problems, such as parity, he dodges. As a campaign orator Humphrey not only avoids even a momentary hard position, much less a permanently precise position, on any major issue, he defends his wishy-washiness with the argument that to be forthright "would be to prove that I'm totally incompetent to handle the job." For this kind of attitude, he has been praised by Republican leader Everett Dirksen as "the professional's professional . . . the modern liberal."

In his four years as mayor of Minneapolis he made an estimated 4,000 speeches, or an average of nearly three a day, counting Sundays. During his fifteen years in the Senate he introduced nearly 1,500 bills and resolutions—a fantastic total for any man. He babbles and exhorts and overextends himself and demeans himself to make even a most simple point. Rather proudly Humphrey admits that he talks too much, and he puts it down to "glands," but one may be tempted to attribute it instead to a hangover from the old days when he was a know-it-all kid entertaining the yokels in his dad's drugstores in Doland and Huron, South Dakota, and later in haranguing the Minneapolis Jaycees. Glib, arrogant, everlastingly front-and-center, Humphrey at first repelled and offended Washington ("I had looked forward to meeting Humphrey," one White House official recalls of those early days, "but my first impression of him was terrible. He was all blather. He bragged endlessly about being mayor. He acted like he had come to Washington to take over"), and to Humphrey's credit, he knew it. Until he crusted over this side of his character and began to be accepted, he was miserable. But the crust has for several years now been wearing rather thin.

The complexities of his ethics were never more accurately

muddled than in his statement to an AFL convention in Cin-
cinnati in 1948, "Not one labor leader has asked me to sell
my soul for anything I don't believe in."

The subsequent years have proved in a startling way, however, the ease with which Humphrey believes in things—as
will be shown later in his wavering on civil rights, and the
shifting of his sympathies between labor and management as
his ambitions mounted. Nothing has made his beliefs so cas-
ual as the vice presidency. In June, 1964, Humphrey, a close
student of Latin American affairs, publicly upbraided Assistant Secretary of State Thomas A. Mann for his hard line.
Speaking sympathetically of Latin efforts to throw off dictator-
ships, Humphrey scolded Mann and other officials in this
country who might be "tempted to return to less venturesome,
more conventional goals, to place less emphasis on reform
and more on working with the established groups to mini-
mize political instability." Humphrey cast his sympathies
with reform rather than with stability, and he warned that
"We may not be able to prevent the emergence of juntas, but
we can and should distinguish between dictators and democrats."

Almost exactly one year later Humphrey was privately defending Mann's hard line in support of the right wing in the
Dominican Republic; and in arguments with his old friends
in the Americans for Democratic Action he was insisting that
we had no choice but to send Marines in to establish a military dictatorship and oust the liberals.

Between the two positions, of course, Humphrey had been
sworn in as vice president.

While Humphrey has sometimes been caught lying, he has
generally avoided falling into the credibility gap; his serious
problem is the intelligibility gap. He says so many conflicting
things, or he says the same thing in so many conflicting ways,
that frequently he simply does not make sense. In 1967, for
example, after visiting Japanese Premier Sato in Tokyo,
Humphrey later said he hadn't mentioned the Okinawa question in their conversation. Sato, on the other hand, remem-

bered clearly that Humphrey had told him President Johnson would be willing to discuss the future status of Okinawa. On another topic, Humphrey said he told Sato that Japan should assume more political and economic responsibility in Asia; but Sato recalled no such admonition being given. Very likely neither was lying; Sato was merely a victim of the Humphrey silly-putty pronouncements that cannot hold a shape.

Sato's mistake was that, whatever he thought he heard Humphrey say or not say, he took it seriously. U.S. newsmen have learned that this is, if not dangerous, at least a waste of time. Not long ago, for instance, Humphrey announced, "I haven't met a hawk in the government." Since the statement was so obviously inaccurate, no responsible member of the Washington press corps tried to decipher what he meant, nor did they feel they were being misled. It was just Humphrey worshiping existence with his tongue; it was a kind of holiness seizure as the spirit took possession of him and his lips and tongue began to move; it was pure glossolalia. And it is nothing new. Speaking to a group of foreign students eleven years ago, Humphrey successfully ignored Franklin Roosevelt's Good Neighbor Policy and his various European treaties; ignored Woodrow Wilson's Latin American policy expressed in the invasions of Santo Domingo and Haiti and his invasion of Vera Cruz and northern Mexico, not to mention his World War I and postwar negotiations with the European powers, ignored also Theodore Roosevelt's stomping about in Asia, advocating either an Open Door or a Busted Door policy, and in the Caribbean; in short, Humphrey just discarded all U.S. diplomacy and world-power maneuvering of the past to tell these students, "We have only had since 1945 to put together a foreign policy. Other countries have had centuries. But until World War II we had no world responsibilities."

His flippant concept of international dealings is, to say the least, stunning. Addressing an audience that understood such insights, the United States Junior Chamber of Commerce, Humphrey in 1966 explained, "Foreign policy is really domestic policy with its hat on." Or, to a union convention in Washington in 1966, "Vietnam today is as close to the U.S. as London was in 1940."

He easily slips his moorings and becomes that most dangerous object, an unlighted hulk. His ways are dark and uncharted, especially in foreign affairs, about which he cares most and knows least. Jack Richardson captured perfectly this wandering side of Humphrey in an interview he recounted in *Esquire:*

> The first direct question I asked then was the possibility of a U.N. role in Vietnam, and, as if in wonder himself, he answered that U.N. officials, after just tidying up their organization's financial condition, were not anxious to become directly embroiled in a war.
>
> "And also," he went on, "that would put Russia on the spot officially. Now that wouldn't be good for anyone."
>
> I wondered aloud that this was an odd position for the U.N. to take since the purpose of its founding had been precisely that there should be in the world a mediating agency to such international troubles. Humphrey looked away at this and with some sadness—perhaps for the simplicity of my remark—murmured, "That's true," and somehow shifted the subject to the safety standards of American automobiles.

Safe worlds, safe cars—as Fulbright noticed, he is interested in everything *equally,* and so he sees nothing wrong in wandering back and forth across all borders in the same conversation, almost in the same breath, although that is not to say in the same thought.

When Humphrey was in South Korea in 1966 as the President's envoy he told officials in that country: "As long as there is one American soldier on the line of the border, the demarcation line, the whole and the entire power of the United States of America is committed to the security and defense of Korea. Korea today is as strong as the United

States and Korea put together. America today is as strong as the United States and Korea put together." Even as diplomatic hyperbole, it was pretty hard to swallow; as a statement for practical application, it would have to be received as just short of crackpot. It fits into the pattern that was best demonstrated within one ten-day period in December, 1967, when he changed from hard line, "wherever freedom is threatened in the world, there we will take our stand," to soft line, "we have no interest in becoming policeman to the world," to hard line, "let those who think we are insincere in our position in Vietnam think twice before acting on that mistake," to soft line, "we seek only to permit self-determination, and if that means Communist rule, that is something we can accept."

Both the saving feature and the disaster of such remarks stem from the same point: five minutes after he has made them Humphrey could probably not remember what he had said. It is a side of Humphrey that can trip the unwary. A couple of years ago Saul Pett, the Associated Press writer, had a long talk with the vice president, during which Pett asked if he intended to try for the presidency in 1972. Humphrey's eyes filled with tears, Pett recounted, and he got to his feet and grandly proclaimed, "It is entirely possible and probable that Hubert Humphrey [he likes to refer to himself in the third person] may not want to be President despite what some people think. But one thing I know. I want to be sure that my granddaughter will be able to read in her history books that" etc., etc. By the time he had finished his oration tears were all over the place and he was shading his eyes. Pett, somewhat taken aback by this explosion of emotion, asked one of Humphrey's closest friends about it the next day. The friend said it wasn't uncommon. Pett asked if Humphrey had meant what he said about not wanting to be President, and the Humphreyphile replied, "I don't doubt at all that Hubert meant and felt what he said *as of the moment*. But I wouldn't count on it."

It is not irresponsibility or hypocrisy. Humphrey is a very

responsible and an intensely sincere guy. He just happens
to be unstable. He wishes everyone so much good that he
is quite capable of promising everything to everyone, and as
a consequence *one* side gets misled and hurt. It is lying in a
way, but it is Humphrey's way, so it is not quite lying.

Up From
The Depression

Hubert Horatio was born into the middle-class Midwestern Humphreys in 1911 in Wallace, South Dakota, and reared in Doland, South Dakota, a town with one Jewish family and no Negroes. It was a town of five hundred population and the Humphreys were important burghers. His father, Hubert, Sr., was mayor, served in the state legislature, and cast his delegate vote for Al Smith at the 1928 Democratic national convention in Houston. Young Hubert, Jr. was a cock at high school: he sang in the operetta; handled the baritone horn in the band; went out for baseball, basketball, football, and the half mile; was captain of the debate team; and he emerged as valedictorian. It was an all-American background, complete with Model T and a dog named Rex.

Humphrey lived in moderate affluence until he was twenty years old, at which time the Great Depression put him to work full time as a pharmacist; even so, he was far luckier than most Americans his age, who had no job and would have no prospect of being able to find or hold a steady job for another eight or ten years. Humphrey often says that the greatest influence on his life, other than his father, was the Depression. The Humphreys actually came through it in good, if touch-and-go shape. Thousands of South Dakota farmers and small businessmen were wiped out but the Humphreys weren't. They had to sell their home, but they held on to the family drug business, moving it to Huron, a larger town, in 1931 for a fresh start. Humphrey was able to stay two years at the University of Minnesota before finances forced him out, and then the family still had enough money to pay his way through a six-month pharmacy cram course in Denver.

He was married in 1936 and returned to the University of Minnesota in 1937, telling his dad he couldn't take the drugstore work any longer: "These dust storms. I'm so tense I'm sick all the time. I get these pains, and I know it's because of the worry. The Depression, the dust, the drought, are wearing me out. I want to move along, to be on my own."

Two years later he had his bachelor's degree, graduating magna cum laude, and went on to Louisiana State University for his master's in political science, finishing in 1940.

Since Humphrey has always claimed that his own political life was the direct product of the New Deal, one might expect his thesis, "The Political Philosophy of the New Deal," to be a profound one. Actually, one is not likely to find a more superficial or a more disappointing appraisal of Franklin Roosevelt's administration. The failure of the appraisal was not that of a green student. Humphrey was on the edge of his political career. This was only three years before he was to make his first attempt to become mayor of Minnesota's largest city; only four years before he suggested to the leaders of the Democratic–Farmer-Labor Party that he would be a good candidate for governor.

Bold and pushy Humphrey may have been, but the thesis reveals a young man of shallowness and confusion about the major political movement of his lifetime—a confusion which maturity and later experiences did not dispel. At one point in his thesis he wrote that the New Deal "has been described by the Marxist as an outgrowth of the same general economic and social factors which gave rise to fascism in Germany and Italy." Apparently Humphrey—who never in his life would have considered himself a Marxist—had forgotten that only six pages earlier he had observed, "The same worldwide economic collapse which brought Hitler to power in Germany in 1933, brought Roosevelt and the New Deal to America." The thesis has other similar flip-flops of judgment, but this is not nearly so unsettling as to find Humphrey seemingly oblivious—in his usual airy hyperoptimistic way— of what had actually been the mood of the country during the Great Depression. "The records of the Depression years," he writes, "reveal no mass violence or uprising on the part of the workers; the only display of revolution was to be found among Midwestern farmers, organized in the Farm Holiday Movement." This is all he says of the great bubbling mood of revolt during the Depression, although his father had even explained why he cancelled all debts to the drug-store one year by saying, "Son, if a revolution comes, ours would be the first store and house they would stone." The bloody strikes, the hunger marches, the forced moratorium of debts, the spirit of anarchy among farmers everywhere (not merely in the Midwest)—he ignores all the many signs that the political soil was no longer inhospitable to radical concepts. "Alien to the American temper and American habits of thought as the Communist credo was," Frederick Lewis Allen writes of this period, "it had a boldness, a last resort ferocity, that might commend itself to millions of desperate men." Humphrey ignores, too, the nearest thing to a revolution in that decade—the organizing of the CIO. To him only Marxists believed that during the 1930's there had been a "rising revolt of the working masses." As for his breezy dismissal of the "only display of revolution" in the Farm Holiday Movement, that was some "only." In northern Iowa the farmers dragged a district judge (who had been imprudent enough to order a foreclosure) off the bench, out of the courtroom and into the street where they produced a rope and prepared to lynch him (his fainting brought them to their senses, if that is the right expression to use). Farmers in several states marched on their capitals to do battle with police and the militia. In Minnesota, Governor Floyd Olson was smarter and invited them into the capitol to address the legislature, which they proceeded to do with ample threats. "Much worse than the Boston Tea Party will happen unless farmers are given relief from debt and tax burdens," one furious old Swede warned the Minnesota legislature. Another shouted, "If we find any senators who are not going down the line with us, we know what to do with them. . . . We won't stand for any more monkey business."

Governor Olson, who knew these were not empty threats, sided with the desperate citizens of Minnesota and threatened to declare martial law and seize anything necessary to help the people if the legislature did not help them. He stood on the capitol steps and addressed the mob of unemployed and hungry who were there for a final answer. "If capitalism can't help you and can't prevent this sort of thing from happening to the people," Olson roared, "I hope the present system of government goes right down to hell!" This was the governor whom Minnesotans today acknowledge to have been their most popular chief executive in modern times, speaking the mood of the 1930's. But apparently Humphrey, swaddled in optimism, had missed the mood almost altogether.

It may be that he missed the mood because he was not living in Minnesota during the governorship of Olson, and therefore missed the culmination of the radical movement in that state; it was a radical movement participated in to a considerable degree by North Dakota, but hardly at all by South Dakota, and this might account for Humphrey's great gaping ignorance of and lack of sympathy for the radicals of the Midwest.

There was a time when Humphrey did not disdain the title of Prairie Populist, but he never volunteered that description of himself. He knew that he was not. He allowed others to call him that because it was politically profitable. He saw himself as a typical as-the-world-turns American boy, a grass-roots loyalist. "That's pretty conservative country I come from," he said not long ago. "We still whistle the 'Washing-

ton Post March' out there. We don't go in for these far-out
things. We don't like far-out art—or far-out politics."

For all its talk about robust individualism and frontier
spirit and the revolutionary spirit of 1776, the United States
has had relatively few radical political movements, and most
of these were radical only by comparison with the very staid
and conservative major political movements. The most deeply
rooted and the longest lived political radicalism came out of
the upper Midwest, which is not surprising when one considers that the Swedes and Norwegians and Finns and northern Germans and Czechs and Slavs who populated this area
in such great numbers were immigrants from and descendants
of an Old World ferment that held in high esteem the philosophy of socialism. The idea of the people taking over the
means of production and the means of marketing did not in
the least offend them. In fact, the people's mastery of their
own economic lives through cooperative ownership was seen
by many as the highest expression of that freedom whose
reputation had drawn them to America. There were some
Communists among these radicals, but the tone of the agrarian and labor radicalism that swept the region in the last
half of the nineteenth century and the first third of the
twentieth century was far from Marxist. While the participants
did not exactly tremble at the thought of a commune, neither
did they press, on a practical basis, for more than some
guarantee against being cheated. They looked upon themselves as the most fundamental of Americans, defending free
enterprise against the monopolists who in fact crushed free
enterprise. They were for state-owned grain elevators mainly
because the monopolistic railroads and the inflexible trust of
the Minneapolis millers constantly cheated the wheat farmers.
The miners, the backshop workers for the railroads, and the
other large laboring groups turned to the Wobblies' (International Workers of the World) radical concept of "one big
union" because the industrialists who employed them looked

upon the laboring man as another commodity, like iron ore
or timber, and not as *participants* in the profiteering side of
capitalism. Generally speaking, both the radical agrarians and
the radical laborers were anticapitalist only because they
were being systematically frozen out of capitalism and made
to exist in a manner more in keeping with Old World feudal-
ism, and they rebelled at this. They were, in a way, more
American than the millers and the industrialists and the
bankers who were their enemies, because they had more
radically cut themselves off from sympathy with the Old
World. They were anti-establishment, anti-European powers,
anti-British, anti-capitalism, anti-imperialism. They tended to
be isolationists. They were more confident of the tensile
strength of Americanism than were the men of great wealth
who controlled the region; they were convinced that economic
democracy could be stretched and reshaped to cover new
problems without being pulled apart.

The farmers and laborers of a radical turn kept their hopes
alive in one political organization after another—the Anti-
Monopoly Party, the Greenback Party, the Populist Party,
and the Non-Partisan League—with widely fluctuating success,
up and down, but mostly down. Prior to the 1930's, the most
successful radical political movement in the upper Midwest
was the Non-Partisan League, which at one point controlled
the lower house of the North Dakota legislature and held all
the state offices except treasurer. When it spilled into Minnesota, it was well received. By 1918, less than three years
after the League was founded in neighboring Dakota, there
were 50,000 dues-paying members in Minnesota, and an official of the Wobblies was predicting that if the IWW workers
(especially strong in the northeast iron range of Minnesota)
and the farmers of the League came to a political understanding, the balance of power in state government would shift
to them. The moneyed establishment of Minnesota was not
unaware of these hopes and they were prepared to beat them
down. Using World War I as a cover, the Minnesota legislature—controlled by the mining, milling, railroading, and

banking interests—set up a seven-man Commission of Safety in 1918, which was authorized to use dictatorial powers to suppress all "un-American" activities. It concentrated on the unions and the agrarian radicals. The Chairman of the Commission, Judge John F. McGee, suggested using a firing squad to thin them out.

Following the war came the U.S. Attorney General's infamous Red hunt, which in turn triggered the labor unions' "purges." In Minnesota, the Republican governor openly denounced the radicals as "bolsheviks." All in all, the radical movement did well to survive at all, but it did, in a political realignment operating after 1918 under the name Farmer-Labor Party, which had enough virility in the early 1920's to elect a U.S. Senator and a couple of Congressmen and throughout the '20's was capable of mustering a third of a million votes. Eventually this party would help carry Hubert Humphrey to the nation's second highest political office, but only after he had helped purify it of radicalism and restore it to the bland two-party mainstream of orthodox establishmentarianism.

This is ancient history, but it is very much to the point because Humphrey participated in a replay of all this. The radical wave building up in the Midwest just before World War I was leveled by a combination of Red scare and war-born patriotism; the radicalism that built up in the decade before World War II was also leveled by a Communist scare and war-born patriotism, and Humphrey helped in this second leveling.

Radicalism's second chance in Minnesota came, as might be expected, with the beginning of the Great Depression. Its chance was caught in the person of Farmer-Labor Governor Olson, who took office in 1930, only the third person to reach that office since the Civil War on other than a Republican ticket. Olson stands in Minnesota history as the master radical, not because he was more so than some of his predecessors but because he was able to promote that side so charmingly and smoothly that he had become unbeatable before the wealthy opposition knew what he was up to. Largely his success in this was not due to shrewdness (although he was certainly shrewd enough) but to his personality. The sod-busters revered him, and the rich men of Minneapolis, with whom he often spent an evening of poker, admired the affable giant who loved his costly booze and cheap women. His interest in the lower class and the needy came naturally; he had grown up in the slums of Minneapolis's North Side. Like Humphrey in a later decade, Olson made his name by fighting corruption in Hennepin County (Minneapolis). He was then district attorney. When his chance came for the governorship in 1930, he was wise enough to pitch his campaign to the hordes hit by the Depression without at first being so extravagant in his platform that he drove away all the conservative Republicans. Once in office, he kept himself tuned to the temper of the people, and since in some Minnesota counties a majority of the people were on direct welfare and not liking it at all, Olson became increasingly tougher, as did the Farmer-Labor Party also. At his second inaugural he laid out the problem as it was speedily unfolding: "We are assembled during the most crucial period in the history of the nation and the state. An army of unemployed, some 200,-000 homeless and wandering boys, thousands of abandoned farms are evidences not only of an economic depression, but of failure of government and our social system to function in the interests of the common people." This was revolutionary stuff. But to prove it was not a slip of the tongue, Olson, a few months later, advised President Roosevelt: "If the so-called Depression deepens, I strongly recommend to you, Mr. President, that the government take over and operate the key industries of this country. . . . If necessary to relieve public suffering the government should not hesitate to conscript wealth."

At home Olson was practicing what he advocated, and pushed through the legislature laws to protect labor against "yellow dog" contracts, laws protecting the farmer with a mortgage moratorium. These, by present standards, are moderate enough measures, considering the crisis of the times. But to the conservatives of Minnesota, Olson was by 1935 viewed as no better than a Communist, although he was far more radical in what he said he wanted than in what he achieved. Still, he stood behind the Farmer-Labor Party, and the FLP stood behind a program, by 1934, which baldly declared that *"capitalism has failed and . . . immediate steps must be taken by the people to abolish capitalism in a peaceful and lawful manner,* and . . . a new, sane and just society must be established; a system in which all the natural resources, machinery of production, transportation and communication shall be owned by the government and operated democratically for the benefit of all the people and not for the benefit of the few."

Olson did not flinch from supporting that statement, although it was noticed that he often "explained" the FLP platform into a more moderate angle, which, however, he could do and still justifiably state, "I am not a liberal. I am what I want to be—a radical." Two years later, however, the most popular and most persuasive governor in Minnesota's history was dead of cancer at the age of forty-five, and the conservative establishment was thereby out of danger. There was no one else around who could swing the populace like Olson, none who could do that and at the same time maintain an uneasy but tolerable relationship with the bankers and mill owners. And so the opposition began to hammer away with the proven tools. Elmer Benson, a left-wing Farmer-Laborite who succeeded Olson in the governor's office, was accused by some FLP members of being soft on Communism, and in 1938 Republican Harold Stassen took up the cry of Communism and defeated Benson with it. (In fact the underground of the Stassen campaign was repeating the anti-Benson slogan, "Communism, Corruption and Jews.")

The radicals didn't know it—because there was nothing unusual about a Republican holding the governor's office in Minnesota, nor even anything especially repulsive about a Republican of Stassen's moderate enlightenment—but that was the beginning of the end of radicalism as a movement in Minnesota. Stassen had little to do with it except that he occupied the governorship at a time when the radicals, if they had still reigned, possibly could have staved off at least some of the great forces that were building against them. But they had no power base from which to operate. And meanwhile their chance of ever obtaining that power base again was being destroyed by a new alignment of liberals and moderates in the Farmer-Labor Party and the Democratic Party, with which the FLP merged in 1944.

The six years of Stassen's term (1939 to 1945) were ones in which left-wing politicians in Minnesota, and elsewhere for that matter, became increasingly suspect. First the compact between Stalin and Hitler, followed by the mechanical warmongering of the Communists in this country when Hitler attacked Stalin, made foreign ideologies more repugnant than ever to the normally isolationist Middle West, and this dissatisfaction victimized some radical politicians who were actually as disenchanted as any conservative businessman with foreign Communism. Too, it was wartime and therefore a time for seeing spies and saboteurs everywhere—and, in this country, since World War I, this has meant primarily *Red* spies. And, to complete the inhospitable atmosphere for radicalism, the war had opened shipyards and defense plants, and had started the railroads to carrying more than hoboes, and had even started a little construction work; people were getting jobs again, and with the new money came a growing indifference to changing "the system."

As they had on other occasions, the men of property could be expected to take advantage of this relaxation to drive a deeper wedge between liberalism and radicalism; in other words, to take the fire out of liberalism. The edge of the wedge would be an attractive, decent fellow who loved everybody except Communists, fellow travelers, dupes, and radicals —and hated them. The edge, as it turned out, would be Hubert Humphrey.

The death of the radical movement in Minnesota, set up

partly by the amalgamation of the Democratic Party with
the Farmer-Labor Party and achieved by the left wing's
being overwhelmed by the Humphreyites, may have been
no great loss to the country. There is of course no way
to say for sure that any influence would have spread nationally from the indigenous radicalism of Minnesota. But on
the other hand there is much to be said for the speculation
of Charles Rumford Walker (in *American City,* his classic
study of the Teamster strikes in Minneapolis in the mid-
1930's). Writing in 1936, only seven years before Humphrey
entered Minnesota politics, Walker saw the traditional radical
base from which a large segment of Minnesotans operated
as offering something of enough value and potential that it
might find root in the national body politic, contributing to
it an undying radical sap and earthy masculinity. Skeptics,
wrote Walker, should remember:

> History has a way of choosing apparently nonstrategic
> sectors of the economic front for revolutionary experi-
> ments. If the experiments are successful they themselves
> become strategic for the whole front. Who would have
> guessed that a clericalist reactionary revolt in Spain—the
> most backward economic sector on the continent—would
> have posed sharply for Europe the question of Commu-
> nism or Fascism? Far less importantly and at a level
> where the forces and objective are more elementary ones,
> the fifty-year story of farmers' and workers' revolt in the
> Northwest may quite possibly have a limited, but stra-
> tegic, meaning for the whole of American economy.

The one thing that would prevent the possibility of radicalism moving outward from Minnesota, of course, would be
the smothering of that radicalism at home. With rather
remarkable foresight, Walker saw that:

> Contrariwise and by the same token, a 'right swing'
> throughout the whole country, *such as a new world war
> might release,* and the whole leftward development in

the Northwest—militant unionization, Farmer-Labor Party
and all—might be swept away. However, for the present
all political weathervanes are pointing left and not right.

Five years later the new world war had absorbed this
nation and the movement was at hand that would indeed
move Minnesota right and would sweep away the radicaliza-
tion of the Farmer-Labor Party. Humphrey was an enthusiastic participant in the antiradical movement. So also were his
colleagues Art Naftalin, Max Kampelman, William Kubicek,
and Evron Kirkpatrick. They could be in the front ranks of
home-front political ferment for the simple physical reason
that they were not in the front ranks of the war itself. They
remained in Minnesota with various kinds of draft exemp-
tions (Humphrey had his physical defects; Kampelman was a
conscientious objector; etc., etc.), while many of their age
peers who might have opposed what they were doing were
elsewhere in military service.

Humphrey's war record, perhaps unfairly, has been subjected to constant attention by his political opponents and
has often been used by them in an effort to discredit him.
Humphrey's first request for deferment, in a letter written to
Hennepin County Board No. 2 on December 2, 1943, was
sought on the basis that he taught two political science classes
to Army Air Corps Cadets at Macalester College. The next
request for deferment was written by an official of the DFL
State Central Committee, dated September 15, 1944, and was
sought on the grounds that Humphrey was a necessary Democratic Party worker. On January 10, 1945, he sought deferment again on the grounds that he was serving as a labor-
relations consultant for the Industrial Grease and Drum
Company and the Sta-Vis Oil Company, both of which firms
had war contracts. The physical defects that won deferments
for him included not only a hernia but also color blindness,
although on the latter one may wonder how anyone who can
see the Red threat and the Yellow peril so clearly could possibly be considered color blind.

Ironically, these young men of Humphrey's circle who were so fortunate as to escape military service were responsible for swinging the merged DFL firmly behind the nation's most militarist impulses during the Cold War years.

What they did was done, of course, from the most patriotic motives and for the well-being, they thought, of the American political process. Having missed the occasion to bear arms against the Fascists, they made up for it in the years ahead by being especially belligerent toward the Communists; in fact, overwhelmingly so. It colored all they did. They were consumed, obsessed, by anti-Communism. They were convinced that once they cleansed the political field of Communism—which, admittedly, they sometimes confused with just plain radicalism—the rest of the democratic process could take care of itself, for there was potential harmony in all that was not radical.

Humphrey once said that his purpose in helping to organize the Americans for Democratic Action in 1947 was "to provide a wholesome, anti- and non-Communist home for progressives." If it sounds like a rest home for decent folks, that's because it was. That has been one of Humphrey's greatest goals in life—to get liberals to stop fighting conservatives, and to get both sides to lie down in some common political haven of rest. "Politics of the old days—when you pitted one group against another—it's out, it's obsolete," he said not long ago. "Hell, I'm an organization man." He can say that now that radicalism seems to be so remote a political influence. A generation ago he *sounded* different. A generation ago, in fact, he said he was going to follow the traditions of Governor Olson. But that was just political talk. That was just to get in, to take over.

Yet considering the things he has done, Humphrey has been remarkably lacking in deviousness. Most of the things he has done can be traced back to a logical influence. Woodrow Wilson has been the steadiest impact on his thinking. This is, he says, the ingrained effect of growing up in a house where the idea of an evening well spent was one in which he and his father would read aloud from the speeches of Wilson. The similarities between Wilson and Humphrey, and between Wilson and the men Humphrey admires, are rather numerous and Humphrey is undoubtedly conscious of them. He is, moreover, strikingly candid about the Wilsonian qualities which he admires. In his master's thesis one finds him praising as accurate and admirable this description of Wilson's progressivism; it is a quote from Herbert Croly's *Progressive Democracy*:

> The slightest question need not be raised as to his sincerity, but his deliberate purpose seems to have been to keep progressivism vague—with a vagueness that is elusive and secretive rather than flexible. His tendency is to emphasize those aspects of progressivism which can be interpreted as the emancipation of an essentially excellent system from corruption and perverting parasites. His version of progressivism, notwithstanding its immediate forward impulses, is scrupulously careful not to be too progressive, and like the superseded reform movements, poses as a higher conservatism.

It describes Humphrey's political career perfectly.

In 1943 Humphrey ran for mayor of Minneapolis and lost. In 1944 he was state campaign chairman for the newly merged Democratic–Farmer-Labor Party. In 1945 he became mayor and in 1948 he was elected U.S. Senator. Those were the steps and he took them fast, en route making an assortment of allies and enemies that people a curiously fascinating but disappointing political saga.

Minneapolis, 1943-1948:
How to Be a Liberal
and a Winner

The Humphrey Story, as artfully developed over the years by Humphrey (who has told it so many times that he undoubtedly believes it) and by his friends and biographers, casts him as the genius who almost single-handedly put together the merger of the Democratic and the Farmer-Labor parties in Minnesota. It is a myth which *Time* and *Newsweek* and similar journalistic conduits have repeated endlessly. The illusion is just as easy to find in liberal magazines such as *The New Republic*. In the March 21, 1960, issue of that magazine, for instance, history is knocked off kilter with the phrase ". . . . the Democratic Farmer Labor Party which Humphrey and his young colleagues formed in 1946," thus adding a false date to a false action.

Humphrey's 1960 campaign biographer, Michael Amrine, using virtually the same wording and exactly the same plot as *Time*, February 1, 1960, put it this way:

"Democratic and Farmer-Labor leaders in Minnesota are probably right when they say that one of Humphrey's greatest political coups was brought off at the start of his career when he succeeded in achieving a successful fusion" of the parties in 1944. Humphrey's other official biographer, Win-throp Griffith, who had been on Humphrey's staff, goes along with the yarn. "He studied the status of the Democratic Party in Minnesota and decided to embark on a private political project," writes Griffith. The project was, of course, to unite the parties. The rest of the legend includes a trip to Wash-ington, a rebuff by the sophisticates in the Democratic Na-tional Committee and eventually a cordial hearing from Post-master General Frank Walker, chairman of the DNC, which got the movement going. The story is embroidered with de-tails intended to persuade the reader that this vivacious young Midwesterner just wouldn't take no for an answer when the welfare of the Democratic Party was at stake.

However, heretics do exist. But before weighing their arguments against that of the established line, bear in mind that before the merger negotiations began in 1943 Hubert Humphrey had only the shallowest of roots in Minnesota; he was a South Dakotan who had lived in Minnesota for about seven years, broken by two long absences from the state, whose only political experience was one unsuccessful race for a city office, and that his mental alliance with the Demo-cratic Party was so tenuous that in that very year he had been tempted, on the encouragement of several rich conservatives in Minneapolis, to leave the party of his prairie populist father and go Republican. *This* is the Humphrey that Art Naftalin and Max Kampelman and other Humphreyites insist handled the extremely delicate task of merging the Demo-crats, who were very jealous of their national party patronage, with the Farmer-Laborites, who were extremely jealous of their greater numerical strength. Even Amrine, Humphrey's Boswell, could not ignore his hero's defects at this point in history: "He had not lived very long in Minnesota, he had not proved himself to be a winning vote-getter, he had no real party experience with either side, and he had no in-fluential power group behind him."

Although Naftalin, for one, believes that it is, in his words, "an Orwellian distortion of history . . . to deny the central and indispensable role that Hubert Humphrey played in the founding of the DFL—he was indisputably the party's chief architect," one must demur on stronger evidence.

The idea of merging the two parties to create a more balanced opposition to the Republicans had been kicking around for more than a decade. After the death of Governor Olson in 1936, the Farmer-Labor Party had fallen apart, shredded by dissension between its left-wingers and right-wingers (not right-wingers in the modern sense, but only compared to the real radicals) and smeared by the Republicans as "Communist infiltrated." As the 1944 elections approached, President Roosevelt worried about the scattered condition of the liberals in Minnesota. The only way the national liberals could be sure of the state's electoral strength would be to put the liberals of the Democratic Party and of the Farmer-Labor Party together, and thus the negotiations were inspired from Washington.

While it takes two to merge, the responsibility of a merger will naturally fall to the larger group, and in this instance that means the Farmer-Labor Party, not the Democratic Party (with which Humphrey was identified). In the last previous state election, in 1942, the Farmer-Labor Party had polled 299,917 votes (37.8 percent of the total) while the Democrats were polling only 75,151 (or 9.5 percent).

When President Roosevelt decided to seek the merger, he of course turned first to ex-Governor Benson, leader of the Farmer-Labor Party. Benson was not close enough to Roosevelt to call him a friend, but they had met several times on government business in Washington and they knew each other well. Now, lest the Humphreyites think that Benson's remembrances might be taken out of context, an exchange with him, even though it entails some repetition, is worth recording.

Q. Could you describe your part in that merger?

BENSON: The President was concerned about carrying the state at that time and he thought it would be good if the Farmer-Labor Party and the Democratic Party could unite.

He asked me my opinion of that, and I told him that were true and it would probably be a good thing. He turned the matter over to Oscar Ewing, Jack Ewing they called him, who was vice-chairman of the national committee, I believe. A New York lawyer. Jack carried it on from there for Roosevelt. He took part in all the negotiations.

Q. When did FDR first get in touch with you?

BENSON: Perhaps '43.

Q. Did Oscar Ewing come out and negotiate in Minnesota?

BENSON: Yes, he was here several times.

Q. How important a role did Hubert Humphrey play?

BENSON: I don't recall he played any role whatever in the merger. He was chosen chairman of the meeting at the time of the merger, but he had no part in the merger.

Q. Who was dickering from the Democratic side?

BENSON: Elmer Kelm was one—he was the state chairman. The treasurer of the Democratic Party at the time—I don't remember his name—he wasn't a very decent person but anyway he took part. And Judge Slen of Madison—he was one of the committee and he was very active. He was close to Ewing and was close to the state chairman, Kelm. I don't recall offhand who the others might have been.

Q. But you are fairly certain Hubert Humphrey had little to do with it?

BENSON: He had practically nothing to do with it. In the end, right at the time of the meeting that really brought about the merger, his position at that time was one of opposition. I think that he and Kelm and this man who was treasurer, I think they thought they had more to gain by keeping the Democratic Party and Farm-Labor Party separate. Patronage, for one thing. He was quite close to Kelm at that time. I think he thought he had more to gain that way. But I shouldn't say because I don't know.

Q. But at least it was your impression that he was against the merger?

BENSON: Yes, I think so. At least he had no part in the

merger. And I think to some extent he was actually opposed to it.

Benson is an old man and he has been sick for years, and he would be the first to admit that his memory is not what it used to be. Taking this into consideration, it still turns out that his version agrees with younger and stronger men, such as James M. Shields, at one time among the three or four most influential men around Benson. Shields's political associations go off in all directions; his brother Art Shields is a well-known staff writer for *The Worker,* the Communist newspaper, and he is the father-in-law of Agriculture Secretary Freeman. Shields recalled: "Humphrey had no real role whatsoever in the 1944 merger of the weak Minnesota Democratic Party and the much stronger Farmer-Labor Party. The prime movers at all stages of initial discussion and final consummation were Oscar Ewing and Robert Hannegan of the Democratic National Committee, President Roosevelt, and Benson."

Theodor S. Slen of Madison, Minnesota, who had been among the Democratic committeemen in the negotiation, added: "Humphrey had no part in working out the arrangements for the merger or for the merger convention. The only contacts made by Humphrey before the merger convention in 1944 were these: In 1943 he came to Kelm's headquarters and said he was deeply interested in politics, wanted to make politics his career, and wondered whether he could get some money for his campaign for the mayoralty of Minneapolis. Shortly before the merger convention in 1944, he went to Washington to ask Oscar Ewing, trouble-shooter of the National Democratic Committee, whether he could not be appointed moderator of the convention, for he needed the publicity that it would give him for his plans to run for the United States Senate against Joseph Ball. Humphrey did a good job as moderator, but he had no part in the steps taken for the new party."

Of course, it must be said that Shields and Benson are not exactly fans of Humphrey, remembering only too well the harsh "anti-Communist" purge of the merged party which he directed later. Their recollections may be suspect for this reason. But Slen holds no grudges, and others, with only a scholarly concern for the period, have reconstructed it the same way. Among these is Millard Gieske, assistant dean of the University of Minnesota graduate school. He stated: "They [the Humphreyites] say Humphrey brought this about, but he didn't do it. This talk of fusion goes back into the 1930's. Sometimes the Democrats would mention it, sometimes the Farmer-Laborites would bring it up. It was bandied about in '42 and in '43, and this was before Humphrey was really in a position to influence anybody. The talk was always there. Humphrey was probably involved in the final negotiations. And anybody who has watched this guy operate knows that once he gets to going, he's right in there. But the merger would have gone through if he hadn't raised a finger."

When Humphrey and his University friends set about to create him as a politician, they looked for allies and they found them in the labor movement. Later, after Humphrey's good showing in the 1943 mayor's race, they would also get money and support from the men who ran Minneapolis, but at first they had to stick with the laborers. These included some Communists and many radicals, but at that point in his evolution Humphrey was quite happy to embrace them. Labor had an organization, it had zest, it had important ties with city hall, and it had some money.

There are many versions of how Humphrey got labor's support and came to power, but the account that sounds right, because it is full of human relations and little logic, goes like this:

Judge Vince Day (now dead) was at one time Governor Olson's executive secretary and was later appointed to the district court bench. He had been of great influence in Olson's administration; some went so far as to claim that Day was the *other* side of the extrovertish Olson, the side with the brains and the imagination that put the Olson programs together. Day was a philosophical anarchist—constantly probing. He was also constantly looking for vigorous young men to bring into politics and keep the bloodline fresh. That's the way he looked upon Humphrey after he had heard him speak at a student gathering at the University denouncing war profiteers. It was, ironically, a peace rally. Day thought Humphrey had a future in politics.

With little more to go on than that one speech and some conversations, Day was nevertheless willing to urge Humphrey as labor's candidate in the 1943 mayor's race. Late in 1942 or early in 1943—the few who were there and remain alive aren't sure whether it was December or January—Judge Day; George Todd, president of the Building Laborers local; Ralph Dickman, County Commissioner; Ed Prochaska, executive secretary of the Pharmaceutical Board under Olson; George Leonard, an attorney and leading socialist; John Boskoe, head of the printer's union; and Bob Cramer, editor of the local labor newspaper, met to decide on the candidate. The choice was between George Murk, president of the musician's union and a state legislator, and Humphrey. The people who were strictly labor were for Murk. But Judge Day—who had that kind of power in labor circles—persuaded them to go for Humphrey, although Humphrey, a political ingenue, had little to recommend himself to this influential group. His main recommendation was rhetoric that sounded like the real Farmer-Laborite stuff.

Among the most powerful, and certainly among the hardest working supporters that rallied to Humphrey in 1943 and again when he was elected in 1945 were the officials and members of the electrical workers union—the union which he, on reaching the Senate, would turn on most viciously and harass as "Communist-dominated." Clarence Hathaway, for example, who had been an editor of the *Worker* during the 1930's, had returned to become a business agent of the United Electrical Workers. Another, Sam Davis, had run on the Communist ticket in the '30's. Without the support of such men he would never have been mayor.

In return for their support, organized labor wanted the one thing of importance that the mayor could give: the chance to pick the police chief. Otherwise the mayor's job was not an important one. In Minneapolis' compartmentalized and decentralized government, the mayor was mainly a ribbon-cutter. But he did have the authority to supervise the operation of the police department, and to the union people of Minneapolis nothing could be more crucial to their peace of mind if not in fact to their physical welfare. Their deep concern over who filled the job had grown out of experiences in the 1920's and the 1930's.

After World War I Minneapolis became known as the biggest scab town in the Midwest. No other group of businessmen in the country were as tightly knit or as determined to resist organized labor; there were 800 businessmen in the Citizens Alliance. They hired Pinkerton and Burns detectives to infiltrate the laboring forces to report anybody who talked of unionizing. It became unsafe to carry a union card; at best one could wind up blackballed from all employment, and at worst one could wind up in the ditch with a busted head.

For a generation prior to 1934 not a strike had even come close to succeeding in Minneapolis. Police, augmented by hired strikebreakers, had crushed them all. Then in 1934, operating under the vague protection of Roosevelt's new National Recovery Administration (NRA), the militant unionists moved out of the shadows; they hit the coal yards in one strike and then the trucking industry. The Citizens Alliance, which had spent $25,000 to smash the last big strike, in 1916, thought they could handle these easily and cheaply. But it didn't work out that way. The first days of the truck strike were relatively quiet, although most retail businesses were crippled or closed. Rapidly thereafter it became real class warfare and there was the threat of municipal civil war. Many citizens believed the city officials who warned of "Communists capturing the streets" and of "Red dictators out to starve the city into submission," and before the dispute had ended—

with the strikers victorious—Minneapolis had seen an unusual sight for that region: police, responsible businessmen, clerks, hired goons and alarmed citizens recruited to the cause of the businessmen, armed with baseball bats and ax handles and bricks, clashing in the streets with striking workers, many of them similarly armed. It was a chilling experience for the city, and both sides in the years ahead adopted, in the main, more subtle warfare strategy.

The treachery of the police department in that strike year, which included decoying unarmed union members into ambush and then firing on them—a year which is still discussed with such freshness in Minneapolis that one can sense the violence of it—left organized labor with a permanent distrust of the police. When Humphrey first ran for mayor, only nine years had elapsed since the Labor War, and it was for this reason that union men backed Humphrey so happily. He would, he had promised them, not appoint a police chief without their approval.

But Humphrey had been making friends on the other side of the track that labor didn't know about; after his strong windup in the 1943 race, the empire builders of Minneapolis were convinced that here was a young man who inspired the voters and, if the country club set talked to him right, might be willing to talk to the voters on *their* behalf. Since the ax-wielding era of the mid-1930's, the employers had quickly adjusted to smoother techniques; the country was changing, and they were willing to change with it—to a point. What the hard stick had not been able to accomplish, they were willing to achieve with soft propaganda: vote American, work American, think American. In other words, don't be a lousy radical. Humphrey was obviously a man who could dispense the message in robust, American terms. After the 1943 campaign, Humphrey was approached by Gideon Seymour, vice president and executive editor of the Minneapolis *Star* and *Tribune*, a spokesman for wealth and property, with the suggestion that he come over to the Republican side. It sounded pretty good to Humphrey. He would never again have to

worry about money to run on, and he would have the endorsement of the unimpeachables. He was not against the
idea. There had been some progressive Republicans in Minnesota. He would not be joining a corrupt or wholly reactionary group. He said he would think about it.

The developments of 1944, however, persuaded Humphrey
and his advisers that the way to power was via the merging
Democratic and Farmer-Labor parties. Back to Seymour he
went to express his regrets, but he assured him that this did
not mean they could not be friends. And friends they remained. In 1945 and for reelection two years later, the Minneapolis *Star* and *Tribune* supported Humphrey for mayor.
Other men of influence were also operating behind Humphrey's election, men such as Samuel C. Gale, vice president of
General Mills; Alfred M. Wilson, vice president of Min-
neapolis-Honeywell Company; David J. Winton, a wealthy
lumberman; and Bradshaw Mintener, vice president and general counsel of Pillsbury Mills, Inc.

These were not exactly men who saw the world through
the eyes of organized labor. But after Humphrey was in the
mayor's seat, it was they, and not union officials, who determined who would be chief of police. Union officials gave
Humphrey the name of their choice, and he turned them
down. Then he went to Mintener and asked him to serve as
chairman of his newly appointed "law enforcement committee" that would name the police chief in a supposedly non-
partisan and classless way. Mintener agreed, with the proviso
that the man Humphrey named had to be a product of FBI
training. This was a cute trick, but it was also rather obvious.
Mintener had attended Oxford with one of J. Edgar Hoover's
assistants in the FBI. He had many friends in the FBI. He
knew that of all the agencies of government, the FBI was
the most vehemently anti-Communist, a tone and coloration
that had been given to the agency as early as 1919 when
Hoover led the notorius Palmer raids against "radicals"—
many of them only union organizers or members—across the
country and began amassing his dossiers on radicals that

eventually developed into a file totaling nearly half a million and was believed to contain some rather lukewarm liberals as well. The FBI agents had found most of their "radicals" by infiltrating labor ranks. Hoover brought this attitude forward unaltered to 1940, at which time he announced that he was re-creating his old wartime antiradical bureau and the secret-informer system that had served him so well prior to the Palmer raids. The next year, 1941, Hoover railed against "... prattle-minded politicians, grabbing for votes with one hand while waving the flag of pseudo-liberalism with the other. . . . That word 'liberalism' is something we should weigh carefully during these dark days that confront our nation."

This was an attitude that the managers of Minneapolis could appreciate. Mintener had good reason for demanding an FBI-trained police chief. And it wasn't as though this left the selection committee with much choice.

There was only one man on the police force, in fact, who qualified: Ed Ryan.

Ryan was an honest cop. He would chase the crooks.

But he also shared J. Edgar Hoover's view of radicals. He had seen nothing wrong in the city's renting its municipal auditorium to Jew-baiter Gerald L. K. Smith, and he had argued that the city council could not do otherwise and claim to believe in free speech. "Some council members," as Winthrop Griffith wrote in 1964 (*Humphrey: A Candid Biography*), "called Ryan a 'fascist' and 'bigot'; a few days later he was 'busted' from the Internal Security Division and sent to the city's Eastside Precinct." To the pro-labor members of the council, as to organized labor itself, Ryan was totally unacceptable. But Humphrey brought him back from precinct exile, accepted him happily, appointed him to the post, and ever since has been calling his choice very wise. As a matter of fact, Ryan was not a strikebreaker. Labor and the liberals had no cause to complain about his actions on that point. But, true to his FBI training, he kept Humphrey thoroughly informed in the immediate years ahead, when Humphrey was

seeking to seize control of the DFL, as to which members
of the party were "radical." And when he needed help in the
identification, he called on his old friends in the FBI, who
opened their files to him. Ryan kept his mouth shut for the
most part during the Humphrey era at City Hall, but lately,
grown old, he has begun to talk enough so that one can see
the sympathies that were motivating him at the time. When
double agent Harold A. R. Philby, interviewed in Moscow in
1967, disclosed that D. Milton Ladd, a deputy director of the
FBI until his retirement in 1954, had "tried to convince me
in all seriousness that Franklin Roosevelt was a Comintern
agent," and when these disclosures of a grotesque mind were
printed in the Minneapolis newspaper, Ryan wrote a letter
to the editor defending his old friend "Mickey" Ladd; but
Ryan did not try to argue that Ladd could not have said such
a thing; no, Ryan's position was that America needed more
men with Ladd's outlook even today to defend us against "the
Red Termites in our midst."

With that outlook, Ryan served Mayor Humphrey very
well in his scrambling over the radicals in the DFL for a seat
in the U.S. Senate.

After the merger of the Democrats with the Farmer-Laborites in 1944, there was temporary outward harmony as the
Benson left wing and the Humphrey right wing joined enthusiasms to help reelect President Roosevelt. Even in that
year, though, there were some tensions. The Bensonites felt
that Humphrey, who was chairman of the DFL campaign in
the state, was spending more time pushing his own career
than FDR's. Humphrey was indeed pushing his career, but
not so successfully as he wanted. Privately, he went to Benson and asked his support in seeking the nomination for governor. Benson, who didn't think a man whose only previous
experience was an unsuccessful race for mayor was quite the
right choice, turned him down. Then Humphrey made a good
bluff, going before the DFL convention to say he didn't *want*
the gubernatorial nomination because he wanted to "go

where our young men are [the war], and you can't deny me that." He never forgave Benson. An ideological tussle was inevitable, and in 1946 the Bensonites won control of the DFL, Humphrey's side having unsuccessfully pushed a former iso-lationist Democrat for chairman. By this time Truman was President, and the victory of the Bensonites made him un-happy, so, when the national Democratic Party sent out some funds to help the DFL candidates in 1946 they were sent to Humphrey for distribution, allowing him his revenge—he held onto the money until a couple of days before the election and then blew it all on useless gimmickry.

To seize the party, however, Humphrey knew he would have to develop a more dramatic cause than this kind of squabbling. He would have to find some evil to overthrow. Borrowing a page from the Stassen strategy of 1938, he and his crowd began to put it around that the DFL was now con-trolled by Communists.

Doubtless Humphrey was convinced that this was so—he would have heard it said often enough by the Minneapolis men of wealth who had helped elect him mayor—but whether or not he was personally convinced, he was a smart enough politician to know that for the sake of his career he would have to wipe away all suspicions of Red infiltration. It did not matter that there were only a handful of Communists in the DFL party and that they were more an irritant than an influence. The problem, to him, was not numerical but psychological. He wanted the party to have the Chamber of Commerce stamp of being pure, 100 percent American. This was highly important to him. His career could be destroyed by this scare issue. It had been used, with the added spice of some anti-Semitism, as the tool to shatter the Farmer-Labor Party in 1938, and the issue of Reds never dies but only festers. In 1944 Humphrey himself had had a traumatic experience. On the eve of the election, one of the county chairman of the DFL issued a public letter saying he was going to vote for Dewey and the Minnesota Republicans be-cause the new DFL was dominated by the CIO, Hubert

Humphrey, Communist sympathizers, Reds, pinks, and pur-
ples. Here was Humphrey trying just to get started in politics and already they were throwing the Red flag at him. He
was hysterical. He rushed to the town where the defector
lived and swore by all the saints of Wall Street that there
was not the slightest taint of Marxism in his heart. That day
he determined he would cleanse the party, even if it took a
bloodbath, even if the cleansing was mostly show and propaganda, even if hundreds of innocents were hurt in the process.

The Humphreyites would pursue their purge to the grass
roots. For instance, James Youngdale, native of a Minnesota
county that was so crushed by the Great Depression of the
1930s and by chronic drought that at one point 90 percent
of the families were on direct relief, a Phi Beta Kappa graduate of Carleton College, a government intern before the war,
a Navy officer during the war—in other words, a loyal, bright
fellow with a future—returned from service to enter politics
and support the rural radical tradition of that region. Youngdale was for Benson and Wallace and their sort, and he felt
that Churchill and Truman were international demagogues,
so Humphrey branded him as a suspicious radical and determined to read him out of the DFL. Youngdale was a tough
fighter, but Humphrey had the resources.

In 1948 Youngdale ran against a Humphrey candidate for
Congress and won the primary, but lost narrowly to the Republican in the general election. Two years later he ran
again, this time narrowly losing in the primary to a Humphrey man. He ran again in 1952, beating the Humphrey candidate in the primary; but this time Humphrey, feeling sure
enough of himself to force a showdown, was determined to
hound Youngdale out of politics. He called together the DFL
officials of that congressional district and demanded that they
disavow Youngdale. They finally did, but sourly and only
after much complaining about Humphrey's use of the whip
and the club. But the upshot of it all was that party officials

announced—and Humphrey echoed their sentiments publicly —that it would be all right with them if the Republicans beat Youngdale.

Apparently, however, his neighbors did not look upon him as the Manchurian candidate. Although he was defeated by Humphrey pressure in the general election, he received more votes in that district than any other DFL politician on the ticket, and the ticket included Orville Freeman, running for governor with the strong endorsement and almost frenzied support of Humphrey.

Speculation in newspapers at the time as to why Humphrey would bring out all his artillery against one congressional candidate wearing the colors of his own party centered around the likelihood that Youngdale was one of those looked upon by Humphrey as a Communist sympathizer; Nixon was coming into the state, and the Humphreyites didn't want to defend Youngdale against any of Nixon's charges.

It is a hallmark of the Humphreyites that they never let up. If they set out to get a man in the 1950s, they will still take a crack at him whenever convenient. Not long ago Mayor Naftalin told a visiting reporter, emphasizing his words with a dour and warning look: "Youngdale—we've known about *his* ideological position all these years."

An auxiliary goal of the purge was to beautify the DFL, to teach it etiquette and manners and make it wholly acceptable in the drawing rooms of the rich in Minnesota. Humphrey, the smalltown boy, wanted to be received. Thus in the years ahead he and his followers turned against not just those whom they deemed too radical but those who were a bit rough-hewn, such as Roy Wier, business agent for an AFL union who was elected to Congress from the Third District. Wier was a courageous Congressman, perfectly willing to stand alone on a vote. He was considered on the conservative side as a labor leader but he voted against the House Un-American Activities Committee at the height of the Red scare. This was not what ultimately defeated him, however. His trouble was, he was the kind of fellow who used to swear when he talked before the League of Women Voters. Altogether the wrong image. So the Humphrey people helped get rid of him.

Steeled for the character assassinations ahead, Humphrey moved toward the critical year of his political life, 1948. At first he disguised his own behind-the-scene role in gutting the left wing. But there were suspicions. In 1947, Dale Kramer, long active in the Progressive farm movement in the Middle West, made these uneasy observations about Humphrey in *The New Republic:* ". . . though Benson and Humphrey groups get along, it is not always without friction. It has been charged that Humphrey prefers the extreme right wing of the old Democratic Party—that in the 1946 DFL convention he tried to force acceptance of one of its members as party chairman. Actually, as in his recent defeat at the Ramsey County convention, Humphrey was lined up with the more reactionary elements of the old Democratic Party who sought to perpetuate themselves in power in spite of the fact that the Farmer-Laborites were in the vast majority in the new organization. Everybody agrees that elimination of the Democrats would be a mistake, yet it is accepted that for years the Democratic organization was a patronage group with limited popular support. Mutterings are heard that Humphrey's aim is to destroy the old Farmer-Labor organization—based largely on neighborhood clubs—and replace it with a personal machine.

"There is also a belief that Humphrey's public and private Red-baiting goes beyond opposition to the Communists and a desire to disassociate himself from them. The customary tactic of Stassen's machine and the press for more than a decade has been to brand Benson 'Communist-dominated.' Many old-timers feel that Humphrey, by his Red-baiting, indirectly supports this campaign while accepting Benson's support.

"Finally, it is claimed that Humphrey's political word is not always good—a charge that would not be recorded if it did not come from sources in entire accord with his general philosophy."

For our purposes, let us momentarily take Humphrey and his planners at their word when they say that they were fighting Communist control. This—1946 to 1948—can thereby be accepted as a test period; if Minnesota "Communists" were in control and if what they stood for was bad for the state and the nation, *this* would be the perfect time to discover what kind of disastrous un-American plans they had up their sleeves. So what happened between 1946 and 1948 in Minnesota?

Nothing. The "Communist-dominated" DFL put forward neither radical candidate nor radical program. Judge for yourself: Their candidate for governor was Harold Barker, a relatively conservative newspaper publisher from Elbow Lake, Minnesota, and their candidate for the U.S. Senate was Theodore Jorgenson, professor of Norwegian literature at St. Olaf College, an intellectual in the liberal tradition; both lost, but they pulled a respectable vote, 40 percent of the total, which is enough to suggest that if they were Communists or fellow travelers the word hadn't gotten around.

To oppose what he considered to be "Communists" within the DFL, Humphrey readily adopted fascistic tactics for his own. In his biography of Humphrey, Griffith quotes a White House aide who recalled his first meeting with the new Senator from Minnesota: "He boasted about some of the tough things he had done with the Minneapolis police. I was shocked by the stories this great 'liberal' told about how he had ignored all the civil liberties to get things done." Undoubtedly the White House staffer had been subjected to some of Humphrey's stories about harassing the left wing of the DFL —stories which were his stock in trade twenty years ago. They were largely true stories. A professor at the University of Minnesota who is a close student of Humphrey's activities in the 1940's (his is a scholarly interest, not a partisan one) has stated that one method used by the Humphreyites to take over the DFL from their left-wing opposition after 1946 was to prepare a blacklist of persons who were to be kept out of party meetings; sometimes, when necessary to enforce the blacklist, two thugs would be stationed at the door and when one of Humphrey's henchmen signaled from within that a person trying to enter the meeting room was on the list, the thugs would toss him into the street, where he would be arrested by a Minneapolis policeman for "disturbing the peace." The police force was under the jurisdiction of Mayor Humphrey, so there was little use in lodging a protest.

The guilt-by-association method of making up the list was interesting, too. Humphrey instructed his aides to read *The Worker*, the Communist newspaper, to see what themes were being pushed. Using these criteria, they were then instructed to keep an ear cocked at the precinct and ward meetings for anyone who advocated things similar to those found in the newspaper. Persons who did were put on the blacklist. Today the Humphreyites, with all apparent innocence, will tell you that it was a fairly foolproof system and that they could easily identify the Communists in the DFL of that day because *they* were the ones who opposed the European Recovery Program—the Marshall Plan.

It was done not solely from the political lust to achieve office and take over a state party apparatus; it was done from personal conviction. As recently as 1966 Humphrey was still saying, "I want to be tolerant but . . . when the Communists infiltrated Henry Wallace's Progressive Party in '48, we fought them. They opposed the Marshall Plan and the Truman Doctrine, and we fought them." The Truman Doctrine and the Marshall Plan are still his historical test for the detection of Communists. This, however, for further political expediency, he attempted to disguise shortly after arriving in Congress, where that criterion stuck in the craw of the Republicans and many conservative Democrats. If Humphrey wanted to get in The Club, he would have to recant obliquely, and momentarily.

Debating one portion of the proposed Internal Security Act of 1950 (the McCarran Anti-Subversive Bill), Humphrey objected to the fact that suspects would be judged as "communistic," or not, depending on, as the bill put it, "the extent to which the positions [they take] on matters of policy do not deviate from those of any Communist-controlled organization, Communist foreign government, or the World Communist movement."

The McCarran system for proving guilt, in short, was the old Humphrey system, but as the following colloquy shows, Humphrey was now attempting to disassociate himself from it.

HUMPHREY: After having read that, I ask the Senator [Herbert Lehman of New York], in the field of international relations and foreign policy, what is the one issue the Communist party raves and roars about the most?

LEHMAN: There are a number of issues.

HUMPHREY: Let us have two or three issues.

LEHMAN: The Marshall Plan.

HUMPHREY: The Marshall Plan. How about military assistance?

LEHMAN: They are against that, of course.

HUMPHREY: In other words, under the terms of this section, anyone who took an adamant position against the Marshall Plan, military assistance, the North Atlantic Pact, any of our major items of foreign policy, would almost stand accused of being a Communist.

LEHMAN: He would.

HUMPHREY: . . . . Is it not entirely possible that some very highly respected, well-thought-of Americans who in all sincerity opposed ECA, who opposed military assistance even by their votes, who opposed the North Atlantic Pact, even by their votes, could stand accused as having not in any way deviated from their position of any Communist form of organization and of the *Daily Worker?*

An excellent question, but he was asking it in 1950, when he was trying to build into the Senate Club and when he was trying to reassure the Tafts and the Byrds of Washington that he did not really think they were Communists, and that they should not take seriously the fact that two years

earlier he had accused his opponents in Minnesota of being
Communists or fellow travelers for occupying some of the
same positions that these archconservatives in Washington
were occupying on foreign affairs.

These whitecaps of change in the Humphrey line, however,
did not reflect a troubled conscience so much as they simply
showed the winds of his ambition were now blowing in a
different direction. Far from being deeply bothered by the
memories of his hand in the smudge pot, he apparently looks
back with warm satisfaction upon the Henry Wallace presidential campaign of 1948 as the great moment, the first great
opportunity for domination, which he and his followers seized
and used successfully to take over the Democratic–Farmer–
Labor Party under the guise of patriotism; it could even be
said that Humphrey and his friends view that occasion as their
most memorable gift to national defense; and it is probably
necessary for them to convince themselves of this, and of the
purity of their patriotic motives, for otherwise it would be
difficult to justify the way they fought that intraparty fight.
On strategic grounds, the Humphreyites deserved to win.
They worked harder, they were better organizers. And in
the best tradition of the followers of Harry Truman, they
viewed ethics and scruples lightly. Their opponents, all drawn
from the Farmer-Labor wing of the DFL, were burdened
with ideology. That year, 1948, was the year of the great
crusade for the F-L leftists. It was the breaking free from the
old two-party mold which seemed, actually, to offer no alternatives. They were buoyed up, bubbling—and clumsy. They
were so convinced of the rightness of the Progressive Party
and of Wallace's candidacy that they failed to realize it was,
as American politics go, and especially in a period when employment was high and economic discontent low, an extravagant route to follow. They attempted to put Wallace on the
ballot under the DFL imprimatur and make Truman run as
the third-party candidate, in the manner that some Southern
states that year would do for Dixiecrat Strom Thurmond.
They lost the effort and many of them walked out of the

DFL to push Wallace on their own; many of the best ones never went back. Humphrey claims he "purged" them as Communists, fellow travelers and dupes. *Time* magazine called the exiles "mainly a mangy crew of spoilsmen and Reds," but most reasonable Minnesotans would, and do, say that they were mostly homespun radicals. After their departure the DFL was swung solidly into the mainstream of the national Democratic Party, which was the only milieu in which Humphrey's liberalism might possibly seem unusual enough to start him toward the top.

The polarization of the fight was between Humphrey on the right and former Governor Elmer Benson, who had been the most influential person in the merger of the parties, on the left. Humphrey's position is most clearly set off by sketching what Benson stood for.

Benson was very nearly an anarchist in his ideas about big business; he was a partaker of the indigenous American radicalism of the 1920's and 1930's, a supporter of La Follette and Wheeler in the 1924 presidential race, and had his roots in the Prohibition Party in a mild way (still alive in Appleton, Minnesota, but ailing these days, Benson has yet to take his first drink of hard liquor). For a few months before becoming governor in the mid-1930's he had served as U.S. Senator, during which time he sponsored the legislation creating the National Youth Administration. As a governor, following Floyd Olson, the first thing he did was cancel the license of Pinkerton's labor-spy outfit in Minnesota. His most constructive act, and the thing that big business hated him most for, was in calling a special session of the legislature in 1937 to increase taxes on corporations and iron ore.

Naturally Benson was called a Communist. Not only did the big businessmen identify him openly as a Red but so also did, and does, Vince Dunne, the old Trotskyite who is a legend because of his leadership in the 1934 Minneapolis Labor War. But as for the latter's credibility, it must be remembered that Benson never got along with the Dunne brothers, that he felt they had betrayed him by calling cer-

tain strikes at politically precarious moments after they had
sworn they would not, and that he rubbed them the wrong
way by making them remove their sidearms and leave them
on a table outside his office when they came to see him. Not
only did the industrialists and the Trotskyites dislike Benson,
so did some Catholics, for when he was trying to push through
the income tax the Catholic Archbishop of that area, who
was from a wealthy family, put it around the Twin Cities
that Benson was "an extremely dangerous man," in response
to which Benson sent word to the Archbishop that he could
"go to hell."

Benson did not have the magnetism of his predecessor,
Olson. But he had his loyal allies, men such as Joe Gilbert,
an old-time Socialist and one of the pillars in the farm
cooperative movement who spent a year in jail during World
War I for "sedition" (he had made a speech against war profiteering), and Marian LeSeuer, a fiery gal who had been
agitating for socialism (such as rural electrification) since the
days of Eugene Debs; after the DFL merged she was elected
national committeewoman and later vice chairman of the
DFL, but eventually sickened of the constant feuding with
the Humphreyites and went Progressive, running herself in
1952, two years before her death, as the Progressive candidate for the U.S. Senate on an anti-Korean War platform.

There was never, either in the 1930's or in the 1940's, any
doubt about where Benson stood on foreign affairs. He considered our declaration of neutrality in the Spanish Civil War
a fraud, since it deprived arms only to the democrats; Franco's
fascists could get all the arms they wanted from Germany
and Italy, who were, in turn, buying all the war materials
they wanted from us. And when, in 1948, Benson turned
against Truman and became national campaign director for
Wallace, it was, he said, because Truman was launching
America upon a permanent militaristic program at home and
abroad: embracing the right wing in Greece and Turkey and
China and Italy, bypassing the United Nations in all important matters, tailoring a Middle East policy solely in terms
of what was believed to be best for U.S. oil companies.

"Whose policy is this?" asked Benson in a speech in March, 1948. "Mr. Truman is the spokesman, but as he has told us so often, his policy is bi-partisan. It is the policy of the two old parties, now in all essentials, one. It is the Hoover-Vandenberg-Dulles-Stassen-Marshall-Eisenhower-Truman Doctrine. But these political figures themselves speak for another group who stand in the shadows. In the shadows, policy is made. The investment bankers whom Mr. Truman placed in political power now make foreign policy in cooperation with the military. Mr. Forrestal, secretary of defense and head of the National Security Council, formerly of Dillon, Read and Company, is today the most powerful figure in the American government . . . America is to rearm. Profits will soar . . . American policy cannot back reaction abroad and permit freedom at home. Mr. Truman calls for unity, the unity of the armed camp. Dissent has already been called treason . . . "

Benson, like Wallace, was subsequently proved wrong about the reasonableness of the Russian leaders and wrong in viewing the Communist take-over in Czechoslovakia as a simple "cabinet change." But these errors of tolerance on the part of the Benson-Wallace crowd have been more than matched, they contend, by the errors of harshness of the Truman-Dulles-Eisenhower Doctrine which built its grotesque militaristic monuments around the world. In 1967, twenty years and $3.5 billion in aid after Truman and his consorts decided to save the Greeks from themselves, the "self-supporting and self-respecting democracy" that Truman promised that land would become as a result of his policy, became a dictatorship instead. The extended result of his policy, nourished by Eisenhower, Kennedy and Johnson, also resulted in militaristic governments in South Korea, Formosa, Turkey, and, to a somewhat lesser extent, West Germany, not to mention the broad military dependency of the multi-nation alliances of both oceans—with that on the Pacific side being used as an excuse for the invasion of South Vietnam.

As for Benson's fears of the military's preeminence in government and of the influence of war industries in this country, these were later to be restated by President Eisenhower, and hailed by moderates everywhere, as being honest harbingers of the threat intrinsic in a Pentagon budget that today is several times higher than it was when the leader of the Minnesota left wing made his warning.

When Benson saw danger in Secretary Forrestal's financial and personal alliances with industry and Wall Street, he was hooted down by the Humphreyites as one who did not have confidence in the American way of life. But when Forrestal's successor, several times removed, Defense Secretary Clark Clifford, took office in 1968, trailing behind him much the same big business and big industry ties (duPont, General Electric, RCA, etc.), the *New York Times* editorially damned this reeking conflict of interest, as did many other responsible journals that could hardly be called radical. When Benson protested the atmosphere of the Truman administration that made dissent a synonym for treason, the Humphreyites called him a riotous malcontent of the far left. The same protests are being made today against an Administration in which Humphrey is a large fractional part of the leadership, but the protests come now as much from the Republicans as from the left; in any event they are never limited to sources that could be dismissed as subversive.

If Benson was correct in attempting to halt militarism, he was no less correct because most of his support came from the left wing, and the trends were no less obnoxious and threatening for being foisted by the party in power; that, of course, is a very elementary political moralism, but it was one nevertheless which the decent go-along Humphrey had no use for. Washington-bound, he was a true believer in the Democratic Party, operating as mechanically as the true believers in the Communist Party, and in 1948 this meant discrediting all leftist notions. (Momentarily he had been a revisionist, joining those who wanted to dump Truman and give Eisenhower the Democratic nomination, but he snapped back into line fast enough to be forgiven by the national party machine, after publicly confessing that "it was one of the worst mistakes of my life.") The cult of Truman was, in its

easy-going, gin-drinking, poker-playing way, as tightly regi-
mented as the cult of Stalin. Anti-militarism was taboo. The
Bensons and the Wallaces had to be so thoroughly smeared
that other potential dissenters within the party would think
again, even if such smearing had to be done in tacit league
with the Mundts and the Rankins and the Joe McCarthys.
From the radical side thereafter, came mostly silence, while
the Pentagon and hardline diplomats pushed ahead.

It is, of course, an oversimplification of the ideological contest between the Bensonites and the Humphreyites, but as
1948 approached, it did come down to just about this: to the
former, Truman stood for all that was shortsighted and mean
in our land, while to the latter Truman was, what Humphrey
called him again in the spring of 1968 (misty-eyed, as usual,
as he addressed the United Auto Workers), "one of the greatest men who ever lived in America."

When the Humphreyites discuss this period, (1946–48) they
tend to weasel. They will tell you that the Communists did not
attempt to destroy Minnesota because they were slyly biding
their time; they will say that the quiet of the period was de-
ceptive; they will inevitably seize the conversation roughly
and divert it away from Minnesota and toward Moscow. But
they are *never* able to get specific and say, "Here, see, this is
typical of the subversive work of the Communists in the DFL
during the period when they controlled the party."

Arthur Naftalin, now mayor of Minneapolis but then one
of Humphrey's closest advisers, was questioned on this point,
of what he saw as the work of the left wing during this
1946–1948 period. (Of Humphrey's three of four most intimate advisers, Naftalin and Kampelman are the most obsessed with the Red theme.) He answered, "Well, they had
a two-year period there where they had a kind of on-again,
off-again attention to the problems of building a party,"
meaning the DFL.

Nothing very subversive about that. More precisely, what
were the issues that divided the right wing under Humphrey

and the left wing under former Governor Benson? "We were divided because the organization of the DFL was important to this [left-wing] group, not because they were trying to build a political vehicle to win elections with," he said, "but because they were trying to build a political vehicle to serve the interests of the Communist international movement. That's the difference." Pressed further to name the issues that showed the subversiveness of the group that controlled in the two years before 1948, he spread his modification: "The problem with the Communists was not that they had a radical philosophy, social and economic philosophy—the problem was they were representing a foreign power. Everything they did, every position they took, was a distortion in terms of what served their foreign policy."

What foreign policy, please, and what issues?

"Well, that's not quite the way to put it. What happened was—to begin with, in 1948 there was this big division—there were earlier divisions but the first big test of this was the Henry Wallace candidacy. This was the big one. Behind the Henry Wallace candidacy was a real division on foreign policy. The Communist Party was opposing the Marshall Plan. Aid to Greece. There was a period after 1946—it was a foreign policy division—it was clear cut. We were fighting as a country trying to export democracy. We were heading into a clash with the Soviet Union. This was what the fight was largely about."

This is inevitably what the Humphreyites will do to you. They will race tiptoe through the 1946-48 "Communist" period, and then leap upon the Wallace candidacy at length and offer it to you as the prize illustration of the evils they were confronted with under the DFL Red regime.

In reliving the glories of the "DFL's Communist purge," Humphrey has embellished the episode so much over the years that sometimes it now sounds as if there was actual door-to-door fighting, with guns and tanks, in the streets of Minneapolis. If one is not jarred back to reality by the recollection that physical disabilities were among the things that had kept him out of World War II, it is easy, hearing him describe that political war, to see him in the streets, wearing a tin helmet and gas mask, mopping up the enemy. "Those of us who had already proven that we were sincere in our genuine liberalism [he once told a *U.S. News and World* reporter], at the same time as we were anti-Communist, had to go out and expose those people, and that we did. We had to fight it out, literally door to door and person to person, in an exposure. [Q. Were you able to proclaim as mayor that you thought they were Communists?] I not only proclaimed it, I went out and fought them and we licked them, hands down."

Anyone who has followed Humphrey's replays of the great DFL war will long ago surely have come to the conclusion that Minnesota was swarming with Stalinists. It is perhaps the fattest and healthiest of the Humphrey myths. But it is also, nevertheless, easily destroyed.

In moments of special candor, and especially when they become a bit rattled by steady questioning, even Humphrey's most devoted apostles will admit that virtually all of the left wing DFL was made up of good Americans. Mayor Naftalin, for example, asked if he thought that there could have been as many as 2,000 Communists in the state of Minnesota in this period (J. Edgar Hoover was then counting about 60,000 Communists in the nation as a whole), answered: "Don't think there were that many in the state. No, there wouldn't be that many. But you see there are a lot of people—you say to me, was this left wing or Communist?—we have in this state—still have—a lot of people who are agrarian populists —real basic down-to-earth radicals. They are against Wall Street, against exploitation, they figure the public domain has been raped, by business and so on. They are right to a large measure. They've heard Red-baiting, they've heard attacks on Communists ever since they were kids during World War I and they just don't believe it. They didn't believe it in '46, '47 and '48. And so they would be aligned in many cases with—I'm not talking about just thousands of good people who were aligned with Elmer Benson and aligned with that leadership. So there was a kind of euphemism that we used— left wing. Couldn't call it the Communist wing. That would just offend a lot of people."

Apparently what Naftalin was trying to say, but for some reason was incapable of saying, was this: the Minnesotans who voted for Henry Wallace in 1948 were just "real basic down-to-earth radicals," almost all good Americans, but they were duped by a handful of true Communists into voting the way they did—duped, in his opinion, despite the fact that the man they voted for stood for the things they stood for in both domestic and foreign politics. Or, to attempt to clarify this foolishness further, the Humphreyites argue unto this day that the exiled wing of the DFL must have been Communist-controlled because, as radicals, they had voted for the most radical candidate in the race. "This is an awful tangled problem to make clear," said the Mayor. "Never could make it clear to Henry Wallace. He found out later, uh . . ." Naftalin's responses agree both in tone and quality with the reminiscences of Dr. William Kubicek, another of Humphrey's close advisers at that time. Between 1946 and 1948 Kubicek, who lived half a block from Humphrey, was the Second Ward DFL chairman; this was Humphrey's ward, the University of Minnesota ward.

Kubicek has spoken of the left wing DFL's activities as being "a Communist-dominated kind of thing, although the known Communists were very few. There were just a few Communists. Only one or two who were open about it, but I suppose there may have been between fifty and one hundred Communists in the Minneapolis–St. Paul area. Many of these people [the anti-Humphreyites] who were with them were just confused.

"One reason the Communists were effective was that we spoke like we had pebbles in our mouth. We were afraid to speak plainly. We were afraid to say this was a Communist movement. Because you could point to certain people and say 'they couldn't possibly be Communist.' And that was absolutely true. And also there was the problem of libel if you weren't sure of it, or even if you were and couldn't prove it. So we devised a way to say it without being brought up for libel. We would say, 'Well, we don't know if they're members of the Communist Party. But if they aren't, they should be. If they aren't they are shirking their dues.' We checked with lawyers and they said that was all right. But it did get the point across."

What issues did you identify definitely as Moscow party line?

Kubicek: "You knew right away if somebody was thumping the table against the Marshall Plan."

What else?

He couldn't think of other issues. The Marshall Plan was as far as he could go. After stumbling for some time, he cut off the questioning with the excuse, "It was almost impossible to identify the issue until you could see the operation. It was just something you had to feel. The issues many times weren't the real problem." Kubicek—a first-generation American out of Czechoslovakian parentage—kept insisting that "Moscow was quarterbacking it," yet the only reason he could give for thinking so was that he had once attended a meeting held by two women he believed were from New York and who were, he believed, Communists.

Although it must have been a bit difficult, in the same year and the same election, to use opposition to the Marshall Plan as proof that Henry Wallace was a pinko and that Minnesota's Republican Senator Joseph Ball (whom Humphrey opposed successfully) was a reactionary, the Humphrey crowd pulled it off. It was one of their most fascinating accomplishments.

It was all the more remarkable a feat when one considers that although Ball was indeed a conservative, on several important issues he comes out, in retrospect, as no more conservative than Humphrey. Ball had, after all, bolted his party to support Franklin Roosevelt for reelection in 1944; and although he had baited labor with investigations and had voted for the Taft-Hartley Act, similar things were to be done by Humphrey within five years after he replaced Ball.

4

The Cold Warrior

Nothing written about these early alliances of Humphrey should be interpreted to mean that he did not agree with the virulent anti-Communists who gave him support and who put him on the road to the Senate. Since it is so easy for a politician to sincerely believe what is advantageous, there is no reason to think that Humphrey, the most adaptable of men, was less than totally sincere. Congressman Don Edwards, former chairman of the ADA, puts this very well: "We are devoted to Hubert in ADA. He is such a nice guy. His problem is he has always been devoted to the theory that there is an international Communist conspiracy and that the movement is monolithic and controlled from Moscow. That's where so many of us leave him. He believes in this right down to the roots of his soul. He is a very honorable man and to say that he doesn't believe it is to say that he is less of a man."

If one's devotion to Humphrey is to survive, this must be accepted simply as a phobia that one must adjust to, for Humphrey has acted throughout his career as though he could hear the hungry grunts of the Red wolves in the darkness, just to the rear, drawing closer, and he has lashed the horses of the Republic into an increasingly hysterical, walleyed flight. He said he favored ripping down the west front of the Capitol—the last remaining portion of the original structure designed by Latrobe—and of tearing up the famous and historic Frederick Law Olmsted terraces, so that there could be cafeteria space in the building; the destruction of that grand architecture was a small price to pay, he argued, if the Congress would thereby create a more American atmosphere within. "Why, as it is, right now, our capitol employees have to line up for cafeteria seats *like queues in Moscow* shopping for yo-yos!" His support of foreign aid was prompted by the Red Threat; and the same is true of his support of education appropriations and of civil rights: they all are part of the ideological Armageddon he feels we are living through. While some other liberals in Congress have fought to curtail the power of the CIA, Humphrey has always sided with the super spooks. "The American people," he said, "feel better because there is a CIA." For months before the news broke that the National Students Association was using CIA money that had been funneled through tax-free foundation conduits, Humphrey knew about it; leaders of the NSA had gone to him to seek his help in breaking away from the CIA and obtaining "honest" money from other foundations. He shrugged off their appeal; to him, the CIA was perfectly legitimate in what it was doing, and in the way it was doing it, because to Humphrey anything is fair in the anti-Communist game. On another occasion he even complained that the CIA wasn't spying enough, and he suggested that Congress appropriate a billion dollars a year, which he called a "modest sum" as budgets go, "to build real dossiers on the top 1,000 leaders in the Communist Party." The information, as he proposed the program, would not be distributed merely among the topmost divisions of the Executive branch but widely, almost at random, through government.

Humphrey's hypersensitivity to even the slightest suggestion that he might be sympathetic to Communist nations resulted in a bit of slapstick roughness in April, 1951, when he filled a recording date in the studios of radio station WINX in Washington. The show was "Meet Your Congress," and he and Herbert Lehman, the old liberal from New York, were to debate Homer Capehart, one of the Senate's more obnoxious ideologues, and Robert Taft on the general topic of what militant policies should be followed toward China. Humphrey and Lehman argued that General MacArthur's policies were bullheaded irresponsibilities that would lead us into war with China. Capehart argued that we should permit MacArthur to use some of Chiang Kai-shek's Nationalist troops in the Korean War, even if it meant triggering a full-scale confrontation with the Red Chinese, and he further argued —in his usual paranoic style—that if Humphrey and Lehman did not favor using Nationalist troops with U.S. troops in Korea, it could only mean that they were basically sympathetic with the Chinese Communists. Instead of treating these comments with the indifference that their source deserved, Humphrey became uncontrollably angry. After the recording was finished, he trooped after Capehart raging and demanding an apology. Capehart (fifty-three years old, 220 pounds, 5 feet 11) brushed him aside. "You accused me of being a warmonger and you called my party the war party," he said. "If you don't like to be called a Communist sympathizer, don't call me a warmonger." Humphrey (thirty-nine years old, 160 pounds, 5 feet 11) kept following him and yelling at him. When they reached the door of the studio, Capehart grabbed Humphrey by the lapels and pushed him out of the studio. (At least Capehart claimed he did). Then (to continue Capehart's version) Lehman grabbed Capehart from behind and spun him around. Capehart pushed Lehman (seventy-three years old, 165 pounds, 5 feet 7) back into the studio. Humphrey by this time had reentered the studio and was busy calling Capehart a sonofabitch. The Sunday punch Capehart was cocked to throw at Humphrey was never thrown—somebody else in the studio stepped between.

After returning to his office, Humphrey issued a statement of his own version of the tussle. For openers, he said that Capehart was a liar. He, Humphrey, had been a gentleman in every way. He had merely gone over to Capehart after the record-cutting and had said, "I deeply resent this type of vilification, character assassination, and malicious unfounded statements—I want no more of it." Following those words, said Humphrey, "Senator Capehart seized my arm and acted in a menacing manner, at which time Senator Lehman tried to separate us and Senator Capehart turned on Senator Lehman." Lee Loevinger, (today an FCC commissioner but then a special counsel for the Select Committee on Small Business), who was waiting for Humphrey, ushered him to the door.

There are elements of authenticity in both versions. Capehart's description of Humphrey's uncontrolled emotionalism sounds right. But on the other hand, given the choice between getting into a fight and using words like "vilification," Humphrey would ordinarily choose the latter every time.

Humphrey's Marshall Plan performance in 1948 was splendidly Machiavellian. He portrayed Henry Wallace as being opposed to the reconstruction of war-crushed Europe simply because he opposed the Marshall Plan way of doing it. In suggesting this, Humphrey was performing an unnatural act with history.

Far from being opposed to the idea of reconstructing a devastated Europe, Wallace wanted to abandon the Marshall Plan only so that he could go *beyond* it and establish a reconstruction fund not supported by the United States alone but by all nations able to contribute, and to have that fund distributed not by the United States but by the United Nations; furthermore, none of the money was to be spent for military material, no political or economic conditions would be tied to the loans or gifts, and the first to receive help would be those nations "which suffered most severely from Axis aggression" (meaning that under his plan West Germany would not have been rebuilt as an industrial colossus until the needs of the western Allies were first served). His were, in short, the principles upon which UNRRA was built; they were sane, decent principles. They were aimed at lessening the division of eastern and western Europe, which the Marshall Plan had increased. Unfortunately, it was a hopeless proposal; it was already clear that Russia was ready to

block any such effort made through the United Nations, and
it was also clear that to attempt to substitute the Wallace plan
for the Marshall Plan would have resulted in an end to the
European Recovery Program *without* a beginning of aid
through other channels. The substitution was impossible.
And it was generally recognized as impossible, just as his
candidacy was so recognized. The question of whether Wallace knew this is not important; the point of his campaign,
the philosophy and hope behind it, was laid out by Wallace
fourteen years earlier in his "Statesmanship and Religion,"
in which he wrote:

> The world is one world. We have our Amoses crying aloud
> over the injustices of the social system but we need in
> addition our Isaiahs who perceive that the Lord is Lord
> of all the earth and that the application of spiritual power
> to a system of nationalistic or class enterprises is a nega-
> tion of true religion. A modern Isaiah . . . would cry out
> against international injustices. He would go to the people
> of the different nations with his message and call for a
> New Deal among nations. He would do this with vigor
> and immense earnestness, even though from an immediate
> practical point of view his message might be premature.

Quite obviously, as Freda Kirchwey, Editor of *The Nation,*
noted during the 1948 campaign, Wallace was "more prophet
than politician." Prophets, unlike politicians, do not temper
their speech to the times, else they wouldn't be prophets. It
was the compulsive message within that had to come out, not
the reaction to the message or the following it developed, that
interested Wallace. It is popular today to say that Wallace
didn't realize that the Progressive Party was a gathering place
for the Communist Party; that is quite beside the point, because if he did know, he did not care. The Communists, after
all, were part of his one world.

Only the frenzied fear developing toward Russia in the late
1940's could have caused the public to be forgetful enough
that it would listen to the anti-Wallaceites who called him a

fellow traveler. As one of the nation's foremost agriculture policymakers, he had advocated throughout the 1930's and '40's nothing more radical in international relations than massive aid to poor countries, which was hooted at by the conservatives then as "a quart of milk a day to the Hottentots," but which today, of course, not only is an entrenched policy of the government but is hailed widely by conservative farmers as a perfect way to get rid of their surplus commodities and keep their income fat; since Wallace's day, conservatives have discovered that global welfare is one of the most capitalistic of government operations. Throughout the 1930's he urged that we increase our military defenses and he was at no time an isolationist. After World War II he did not side with Secretary of Treasury Henry Morganthau in seeking to keep Germany industrially weak (which was, coincidentally, the Communist advice), but rather he went along with Secretary of War Henry Stimson in urging that Germany be helped, in its turn, to readjust to an industrial world. He did not ask for vengeance against the Nazis. This hardly made him pro-Nazi. But then, at the same time, he urged that the United States make greater efforts to get along with Russia, and for this he was widely damned as pro-Red. One will search his Madison Square Garden Speech of September 12, 1946, in vain to find anything in it even remotely "radical" enough to justify President Truman's kicking him out of the cabinet, which was the result of that speech. "We must earnestly want peace with Russia—but we want to be met halfway. We want cooperation. And I believe we can get cooperation once Russia understands that our primary objective is neither saving the British Empire nor purchasing oil in the Near East with the lives of American soldiers. We cannot allow national oil rivalries to force us into war. . . ."

That was Communistic? If not, perhaps this was: ". . . the Russians should stop conniving against us in certain areas of the world just as we should stop scheming against them in other parts of the world. . . . Under friendly peaceful competition, the Russian world and the American world will gradually become more alike." Which, of course, is exactly what has been happening at a fast pace.

"I am neither . . . anti-Russian nor pro-Russian," Wallace said. ". . . The tougher we get, the tougher the Russians will get." Billions of dollars later, that is exactly what happened. "Russia had no nuclear weapons," recalled retired Major General David M. Shoup, former commandant of the Marine Corps and a Medal of Honor winner. "We encircled her with nuclear bombs and missile bases. . . . By so doing, we gave her the greatest psychological booster possible. . . . From here it was easy to get these people to forgo butter for guns. . . . They did it. They have the weapons. Weapons enough to shove everything above ground in western Europe, including the British Isles, right out into the Atlantic Ocean. And enough of the transcontinental weapons to clobber America from coast to coast and produce unacceptable destruction. . . ." So peaceful coexistence with the Soviet Union, which Wallace once advocated, finally became not only respectable (Humphrey is among its advocates) but necessary for survival.

With an atomic bomb monopoly and an economy that was actually strengthened by World War II, the United States could have risked a more cooperative attitude toward the Russians after the war without endangering national security. But President Truman abruptly canceled Lend-Lease to the Soviet Union, which lost 20 million citizens during the war and had its economic structure battered by the German invasion. The wartime allies soon became peacetime belligerents, each trying to prove to the other that they wouldn't be pushed around. Russian nationalistic behavior was equated with the ideology of revolutionary Communism.

"Throughout Russian history real circumstances have justified the fear by which the Russians have been governed," Louis J. Halle wrote in *The Cold War as History*. "For ten centuries they have survived the greatest trials experienced by any people in the world today only because they have been so governed." Russian expansion, since the days of Ivan the

Great, has been primarily a defensive expansion to compensate for a lack of natural defensive frontiers that encouraged a succession of foreign invasions, Halle explained. Truman, with the support of Humphrey and many other liberals, declared a worldwide crusade against Communism in response to Russian maneuverings to assure friendly regimes in eastern Europe and despite Stalin's coolness to Communist revolutions when he feared that he couldn't control them (Stalin delayed aiding the Chinese and Yugoslavian Communists until their victories seemed certain). The sad truth is that the get-tough policies which Humphrey and other liberals helped shape twenty years ago against the Soviet Union, probably delayed the rise of independent Communist states in eastern Europe pursuing their own national interest, which is happening today.

To drum up essential popular support for the holy war against Communism, it was necessary "to scare hell out of the American people," in the words of Republican Senator Arthur K. Vandenberg of Michigan, by convincing them that Communism was a monolithic evil which would socialize Mom's apple pie if Americans didn't arm themselves and do battle around the globe. Humphrey liberals provided the leadership that forged this bipartisan foreign policy. By mistakenly concluding that all Communists are brothers until the bitter revolutionary end, the Humphrey liberals set in motion forces which doomed the very domestic reforms they championed, threatened traditional American freedoms, and thwarted the development of an enlightened U.S. foreign policy that some liberals later came to champion.

On the evening of June 26, 1950, in Blair House across Pennsylvania Avenue from the White House, President Truman made the decision to intervene with force in the Chinese civil war as part of the American strategy in responding to the Korean War—the interposing of the U.S. Seventh Fleet between the victorious regime of Mao Tse-tung on the Chinese mainland and the defeated Nationalist regime. The military necessity cited for such a momentous action—that impoverished China, staggering from thirty-nine years of civil war and World War II, otherwise might invade Japan—was so outlandish as to suggest that Congress should require the Secretary of Defense to be a psychiatrist.

Before Truman's decision, Hubert Humphrey was urging the Senate to get its mind off Formosa ("little old Formosa," he called it) and think of India. ". . . I want to stop Communism," Humphrey told the Senate on January 5, 1950, "and I say that if we lose the south part of Asia, if we lose the Malay Peninsula, if we lose Burma, if we lose India, we shall have lost every hope that we ever had of being able to maintain free institutions in any part of the world. . . . Rather than fleets for Formosa, let us have some food for India." Those remarks reflect both Humphrey's belief in American omnipotence ("if we lose") and his view of foreign affairs as a gigantic game of dominoes (as Burma goes, so goes Maine). After Truman's decision, Humphrey, always a partisan trooper, ate his words about no fleets for Formosa, cheered the new party line and even demanded faster action. "I wish to know why there has been delay in getting the fleet out of mothballs, why so long has been taken, and why only one or two vessels at a time have been made ready," he told the Senate on July 12, 1950, seven months after his "little old Formosa" speech.

Humphrey's enthusiasm for the Cold War—although it soon shifted back to Europe almost exclusively—never waned during those tense times when the mildest dissent was considered disloyal. He didn't challenge our tragic stretching of the U.N. mandate to protect South Korea to include liberating North Korea. The Chinese Communists (through India) clearly warned the United States that they would intervene if American troops entered neighboring North Korea. The Chinese did just that and thousands of American soldiers needlessly were killed in salvaging South Korea for the second time.

Intervening to save Chiang Kai-shek on Formosa and blindly allowing the Korean conflict to become a Chinese-

American war eliminated any possibilities that the United States could develop diplomatic relations with the Chinese Communists, thus forcing them into the uncomfortable embrace of the Soviet Union for a decade before their angry separation. The tragedy is that U.S.-Chinese relations might have been different. ". . . American leaders were aware that the Chinese Communists, after a long debate, had concluded in September, 1944, that they preferred to work with the United States rather than with Russia in the future development of China," historian William A. Williams wrote in *The Tragedy of American Diplomacy*. This is plausible in view of Stalin's indifferent support of the Chinese Communists and the nasty row that later developed between the two countries (after all, the Soviet Union includes territory that historically belonged to China). "The alienation of the friendship of the great and wonderful Chinese people will surely vie for decades to come as the greatest blunder this country ever made in her relations with other nations, unless the final results from the Vietnam commitment overshadow it," commented General Shoup.

While the Truman Administration, with Humphrey's support, took the military steps in China's back yard that were to assure its belligerent isolation from the United States, the Cold War began to backfire at home. The anti-Communism crusade abroad inevitably led to McCarthyism at home. The search for scapegoats and the anti-intellectualism that resulted drove practically all of America's China experts from the State Department without a murmur from Humphrey.

While Humphrey did use anti-Communism for political advantage and also because of a sincere though warped fear of what the "monolithic global Communist conspiracy" was plotting against his homeland, it must be said that he was never an outright kook on the subject, and, in fact, he retained enough clarity of vision to actually speak out in an effort to stop some of the kookier and some of the more vicious uses of anti-Communism.

When the *Reader's Digest,* in 1950, branded the rigidly anti-Communist ADA as a tool of Communism, Humphrey protested to DeWitt Wallace, the *Digest's* editor, asking for a chance to either write a letter or a full-scale article in reply. The *Digest* turned him down and Humphrey denounced it in a Senate speech. (It was an especially irritating experience for Humphrey because he thought he had something of an in with the Wallaces. DeWitt Wallace's father, John Wallace, was president of Macalester College, where Humphrey used to teach. In fact, Humphrey was a professor hired by funds from the Byron Foundation Funds, which was set up by the *Digest's* editor.)

In 1956 (having had a year's respite from McCarthyism) Humphrey praised Ike's decision to send aid to Ceylon despite its being ruled ineligible under the Battle Act, which denied U.S. aid to countries that dealt in strategic material with the Reds; Ceylon, starving, had in 1952 agreed to swap rubber for rice from China.

And in the 1950s, when many in Congress felt that no Communist nation, much less Red China, should even be spoken to, Humphrey was saying that the policy of forbidding passports to U.S. newsmen who wanted to visit China was stupid and that equally stupid was the policy of forbidding the entry of Red Chinese newsmen into this country. In typical Humphrey-esque, he offered, "I am willing to admit the abominable snowman from the mountains of Nepal if he can get over here."

When the nuts were accusing the National Council of Churches of being a front for subversive activities, Humphrey ridiculed them. When the witch-hunters began to get after Oscar Ewing, FDR's aide who had supervised the merger of the DFL, Humphrey publicly came to his defense. And in the same year, 1950, when the vested interests that had destroyed Senator Claude Pepper in Florida moved into North Carolina to smear Senator Frank Graham as a Communist, Humphrey spoke out: "If a person joins an organization which is dedicated to noble purposes, if that organization has a few scoundrels in it, and a person is being accused of being a Communist, the effect is to destroy the heart of America, to destroy humanitarian America. There is nothing more brutal and more selfish than aristocratic respectability and acceptability." (One cannot but wonder, when Humphrey applies tolerance to North Carolina that he seldom showed in Minnesota, to what extent such statements are made in expiation of his awareness of what he had done at home).

But perhaps Humphrey's most dramatic defense of a decent government official against a concerted smear campaign was in 1949, when Leland Olds was being considered for reconfirmation to another term on the Federal Power Commission. Olds, one of the best commissioners to serve on that body at any time in its history, had saved millions of dollars for the American consumer by his decisions on rate questions. But he had also gained the deep and bitter enmity of the oil and gas companies, who now wanted to get rid of him and were willing to do so by bringing up some of Olds's radical writings during the 1920's. The handmaiden of the oil industry's attack was Senator Lyndon Johnson, and he was eventually successful in leading the Senate into voting against the reconfirmation of Olds. But first came some stirring speeches in Olds's behalf, and none was more stirring than Humphrey's. It was not an especially courageous position to take; it was quite obvious that Olds was being hatcheted by the oil and gas interests, and even such conservative newspapers as the Des Moines *Register* and the Kansas City *Star* expressed editorial indignation at the slanderous attack. The fight really was not—as the line of the vote indicated—between liberals and conservatives but between oil-state senators and those who were not under the influence of oil and gas money. Minnesota is among the states that can be independent of such pressure, and so it was natural for Humphrey to side with Olds against the hatchetmen. Moreover, some powerful farm and labor groups in Minnesota were very much on Olds's side, so it was even expedient for Humphrey to side with him, too. Still, he deserves a little special praise since he was so hypersensitive to the Red scare and that was the *public* presentation of the Olds case.

Humphrey came to his assistance in his most flamboyant, evangelical style:

> There is not one iota of evidence that he was ever a Communist. In fact, he is a devoted American. There is evidence that he had the courage in the 1920's to stand up and say that he did not like the plundering of the stock market. He had the courage to say that he did not like the way the American enterprise system was refusing to recognize human rights. In the 1920's the American enterprise system was refusing to recognize human rights. In the 1920's the American enterprise system should have been criticized, and anyone who conclusively criticized it should have a crown of diamonds. If there is any room in heaven for a politician, the politician who will be in heaven is the one who had the courage to stand up and condemn the exploiters of child labor and of adult labor, the exploiters of the widows who put their money into phony stocks. If Mr. Olds had the courage to stand up in the 1920's and say that he did not like that kind of rotten business practice, God bless him. Those who should be on trial tonight are those who sat serenely and did not raise a finger of protest when millions of people were robbed, families were broken, homes were destroyed, and businesses were bankrupted. All they did was to talk about some kind of business confidence, and prosperity around the corner, and split up the loot. If there is any divine justice those men will fry, and Mr. Olds will have a crown. If the Senate is going to crucify a man because of his loyalty, if the Senate is going to drive that man down into the dirt, and deny him a chance to render public service, because of his faith in his God, his country, and himself, then I say the Senate of the United States has "gone off the deep end" in behalf of what I call political double talk and pressure from pressure groups.

Given half a chance, Humphrey's sense of fair play will counterbalance his fear of Communists; seldom is it given half a chance, especially in international affairs, but fair play once more came through in 1959, after Castro's takeover. He was not one who jumped on Castro at once. In fact, in April of that year he said that "To millions of Cubans he symbolizes their hope for a better life" and he said that "he has surrounded himself in his cabinet with a number of honest, capable men, several of whom are accompanying him to Washington." About the specter of Communism, Humphrey said merely, "Dr. Castro's labors are complicated by the machinations of the International Communists. . . ." But so that it would be understood that he was not seeing too much in that, Humphrey added that other governments, including Batista's, had also "found it convenient to play ball with the Communists." He called for "understanding and help" for the Cubans and for Castro. It was one of Humphrey's tragically rare moments of tolerance for far-leftists in other countries.

More often, Humphrey frittered away his influence through organizations such as the Committee of One Million, an extremist group dedicated to keeping Red China out of the United Nations. It is a sad waste, but it has its amusing aspects, too, seen nowhere better than on the scroll that used to hang in his office. It was from General Edwin Walker, the eminent right-winger, and it was inscribed "To Hubert Humphrey, defender of democracy at the Berlin wall."

On Monday, March 17, 1952, Senator Humphrey, flanked by his legislative counsel, Max Kampelman, and other staff members, stalked jovially—he and his staff were, in fact, the only accomplished *jovial* stalkers on Capitol Hill in that era— into chambers of the Subcommittee on Labor and Labor-Management Relations where he assumed the chairman's seat and opened the singularly unproductive investigation of "Communist domination of unions and national security" which was to run on for ten days, in a widely scattered fashion, into July. Washington paid scarcely any attention to the hearings. On the last day Humphrey observed with irritation, "This is the first day on which we have had more than two members of the press here, and they did not have any other place to go today, to be very candid. I am not being unkind to my friends of the press, but it has been literally true that we have held these hearings with a corporal's guard." He could also have pointed out at the conclusion of the hearings that on only *one* day did as many as three of the seven-man subcommittee show up, that on seven of the ten days he was the *only* member of the subcommittee on hand, and one day even he stayed away.

The spook under study—subversive Communism in labor—contrary to the surface impression left by the demagogues and the headlines, was obviously not a problem that the more intelligent crust of the public or of Congress viewed with much alarm in 1952. The *formality* of being frightened by "Reds" was still very much in vogue, but most men who had enough wit to obtain a seat in the United States Senate were beginning to see, by 1952, that the Communists had other things to do than lay plans for the dynamiting of U.S. industrial centers and similar mischief and that the stupidities of Russian foreign policy would probably be sufficient to protect us from our own stupidities. Humphrey, however, had no such inward assurance. He said that he quite agreed, fulsomely and emphatically, with McCarran and Rankin (those men of loathsome reputation in liberal circles) that there was a threatening conspiracy in this country. Also, it must be added, without emphasis, that the hunt for Commies was a standard vote-getting political maneuver in the early 1950's and Humphrey was coming up for reelection in another year and a half. Moreover, he did not have to guess at the possible tactics of the opposition when he ran for reelection, since already in 1952 the Republicans were showing, in the presidential campaign, the skill and variety with which they could concoct evidence of the Democrats' being "soft on Communism." We were fighting the Red and Yellow

Peril in North Korea, Russia was making snotty remarks, the
$60,000,000,000 Pentagon budget had the nation in a fat and
bellicose mood, and the McCarran-Walter Act was obviously
going to pass, despite President Truman's veto, which showed
that the mood of the country—or at least of the lower-middle-
class portion of the country which Congress represented—
was in a mood to keep out all future Saccos and Vanzettis.
To Humphrey, it was a political moment to move against the
ragged army of Commie scarecrows. Thus, a combination of
honestly frightened goosebumps and calculated political
maneuvering brought him to open the hearings with the old
outdated scare of a physical threat: "We are starting our
hearings on Communist-dominated unions with only one
preconception; it is this: There are certain Communist-dominated unions in the United States operating in defense industries, and we must face up to what this fact means for our
national security."

Well, just what *did* "this fact" mean; what was he getting
at? Nothing, it seemed, that had anything to do with this
country. He introduced two newspaper clippings datelined
Berlin and two datelined Vienna, all implying that the Communist "world network" was preparing to cripple the West's
military efforts by wildcat strikes and similar slow-down
devices. Unfortunately for Humphrey's thesis, the most dramatic wildcat strike in this country in recent months had been
pulled by the International Longshoremen's Association
(AFL), which was so right wing that it was practically fascist.
Its head was the infamous Joe ("King") Ryan, a dock muscle-
man allied with corrupt politicians in New York City whose
concept of the purposes of organized labor was about on the
same level as that of his philosophical heir, Jimmy Hoffa of
the Teamsters, which is to say, labor was something to use
for personal aggrandizement and wealth, not for some mystic
world conspiracy.

But Humphrey plunged ahead, notwithstanding a drought
of evidence: "Nor is there any doubt in my mind that Communists seek to use the unions as systems of power to promote

Soviet Russia's foreign policies. . . . I speak my opinions with a considerable background and conviction" (meaning, apparently, his rift with the unions in Minnesota).

There had been suspicions among some union officials before the hearings opened that Humphrey was playing his part in a program approved by employers and by the more conservative unions to discredit and weaken the militant unions; the suspicions were that Humphrey's hearings would make it easier for the conservative unions to raid industries held by the militants. The worried militants pointed to an interview Humphrey had given to the business-oriented *U.S. News and World Report.* In that interview he had stated his "certainty" that the nine unions recently banished from the CIO were "Communist-dominated." He was apparently unwilling or unable to conceive of a plain old-fashioned power struggle. He proudly told of his role in placing the secret CIO proceedings against these unions in the *Congressional Record* so that charges—many of them unsupported—that had been made against the expelled unionists could be repeated publicly without fear of a libel suit. The interview at this point is a strange mixture of childish naïveté and childish viciousness:

Q. All of these documents about the CIO proceedings and trials now have become "privileged," haven't they, and the papers can now reprint those documents without any fear of libel action?

A. That is correct. This is an official Senate document, and may I say I had the fullest cooperation of the officers of the CIO in obtaining these reports. [Hardly a remarkable achievement, inasmuch as Phillip Murray and other officers of the CIO were in a blood feud with the expelled unionists.]

Q. But at the time of the CIO trials a lot of this stuff made public was not "privileged," so that anybody could have sued if he had had a case?

A. That is correct.

Q. Isn't this one of the advantages of "congressional immunity"?

A. Yes, indeed.

In that interview Humphrey conceded that he was contemplating several anti-Communist tactics of a strong-arm nature (later he denied that he was really giving them serious consideration). He said he wanted the Justice Department to be as tough on citizens of this country as the Department of Immigration was on people trying to enter the country. He thought it might be a good idea to put suspect unions on the Attorney General's list; and thus was posed the specter not only of a lengthening list of organizations made anathema simply through the whimsy of a government clique, but now also, if Humphrey's concept had come into being, a list which made a machinist or an electrician as "un-American" as a night-riding Klansman, simply because of membership in a proscribed union. But Humphrey's pulsating pogrom had more: The non-Communist oath provisions of the Taft-Hartley Act, he said, were far from a sufficient safeguard; stricter screening procedures should be set up to hound the liars and to harass the fudgers. He wanted also to "explore" the idea of barring certain unions from representing workers in plants even indirectly related to defense production. In fact, he was considering the "possibility" of excluding some unions from "the privileges of collective bargaining" because of their political beliefs. Then he went on hurriedly in a vain effort to sound moderate: "That doesn't mean that you could drive out the union as such. It doesn't mean that you could prevent them from organizing. But when you organize, you cannot enjoy the privileges provided by the National Labor Relations Act, that's all." Or, to put it more bluntly, in his words: "It could be a matter of public policy and could be a matter of public law that a union which, for all practical purposes, is a political organization controlled by and under the leadership of proven and known members of the Communist Party, and *following a line which one is able to identify as the Communist line,* that even if that union gets a majority, it shall not be given bargaining status in terms of a collective-bargaining contract."

It was the kind of nasty blackballing for "party-line suspicions" that only the most conservative businessmen were urging. Officials of General Electric and Westinghouse, for example, had earlier proposed exactly the same thing that Humphrey was talking about. But for all its vengefulness against the outcasts, the CIO did not want Humphrey to go that far in his recommendations, and after the interview he became noticeably defensive on the subject, saying that he only meant the subcommittee would consider all sorts of remedies. Coupled with the basic repugnance of labor leaders to the anti-Communist "possibilities" proposed by Humphrey was the fact that the AFL and the CIO were in no mood to adjust to witch-hunting, inasmuch as they were soon to be in the throes of readjusting to new leadership, and Humphrey, though he listened to big business, then listened more closely to big labor. Four months after the hearings closed, both CIO President Philip Murray and AFL President William Green died, succeeded by Walter Reuther of the United Automobile Workers (CIO) and by George Meany, moving up from AFL secretary-treasurer to take the presidency. Reuther and Meany said they could handle their own Communist baiting, and Humphrey was only too happy to leave it to them because on the one hand he was extremely close to Reuther and on the other hand it would have been impossible to make the general public think that Meany, who marched through life humming a Sousa tune, could not keep the AFL conservative. The Humphrey hearings, therefore, resulted in no legislation.

It was just as well for Humphrey that the press had paid so little attention to his hearings; he had not, in the final round, fared well at all. He had run up against contentious James J. Matles, director of organizations for the United Electrical, Radio, and Machine Workers of America—better known simply as UE—and Humphrey was no match for him.

Humphrey had received the support of the UE of Minneapolis in his campaigns for mayor and he had received the support of the several thousand UE members around the state when he ran for the U.S. Senate in 1948 and in none of these instances had he spurned their help; but in the early summer of 1948 he had met privately with CIO President Murray and several of his executives and agreed that he would launch a full-scale attack on what Humphrey called "left-wingers, Communist-fronters and open members of the Communist Party" in Minnesota with the understanding that Murray, in turn, would protect his flanks and give him full support. Some of Humphrey's most vigorous attacks thereafter were on the UE.

It is certainly true that the UE was leftish and that it had Communists in its ranks, but there is also reason to believe that much of the abuse it received at the hands of the professionally patriotic labor leaders in the CIO was merely part of the strategy of an internal power struggle, although Humphrey himself was willing to disregard this and take the unrelenting position that "there's no doubt at all in my mind that . . . the United Electrical Workers are Communist-dominated." In 1949 the UE had been kicked out of the CIO and a rival union blessed by the CIO (the International Union of Electrical, Radio and Machine Workers) was organized, headed by James B. Carey, secretary of the CIO. Carey had been president of the UE. Thereafter there was an intense struggle for membership between the UE and the new IEU, and the charge of "Communist domination" played an important part in the struggle.

In 1940, when Carey was still president of the UE and that union was in jurisdictional war with the corrupt International Brotherhood of Electrical Workers, he was dodging the same charges that later he was dishing out: in 1940 he observed that, although the House Committee on Un-American Activities (then headed by Martin Dies) had accused the UE of being Communist-controlled, "There is no control by Communist leaders in our national union. There are Communists, no doubt, among our members . . . [because] we discriminate against no worker for reason of race, creed, color, or political belief. To deny any worker equality of participation would be a denial of democracy and the very life of unionism"—the *precise* argument he was denouncing eight years later, having been finally beaten into orthodoxy by the Dies committee and other heavy pressures from within and from without the labor movement.

This Matles pointed out to Humphrey, after which he checked off others in big labor who had caved in, such as Walter Reuther, who, on April 14, 1941, had declared: "Many years ago in this country, when the bosses wanted to keep the workers from forming a strong union, they started scares of various kinds. One scare the bosses raised was the Catholics against the Protestants. Another scare they used very successfully was the American-born against the foreign-born .... All that is played out now. It has been worked too often. So now the bosses are trying a new stunt. They are raising a new scare, the Red scare. They pay stools to go whispering around that So-and-so, usually a militant union leader, is a Red. . . . So let's all be careful that we don't play the bosses' game by falling for their Red scare. Let's stand by our union and our fellow unions. No union man worthy of the name will play the bosses' game. Some may do so through ignorance. But those who peddle the Red scare and know what they are doing are dangerous enemies of the union."

Only four years later, Matles reminded the committee, Reuther was using the Red scare to seize control of the United Auto Workers in a violent internal struggle.

CIO President Murray resisted the Red scare gimmickry longer than most, Matles pointed out, and even at the 1946 convention of steel workers was saying: "As a democratic institution we engage in no purges, no witch hunts. We do not dictate a man's thoughts or beliefs. . . ."

But those days were past, as a result of countless purges across the nation similar to the one Humphrey had helped launch in Minnesota. It was no longer safe to be tolerant of far-left views. The UE leadership had backed Wallace in 1948; so Humphrey suspected all its actions thereafter. John Small, chairman of the Munitions Board, testified at the Humphrey hearing that "there is not the least bit of doubt that if the policy of the Soviet Union called for strikes in various industries in the United States, then the leadership [of UE] would subjugate the membership to a strike."

Matles, with very little excess, called Small a "damnable liar," and then destroyed Small's argument by pointing out that during the Lend-Lease period of 1940, when Russia and Germany were allies and the Communist Party in this country opposed our helping England and France, 475 UE members at a Brooklyn torpedo plant voted to strike but delayed the strike on his advice. He produced a clipping from the newspaper *PM* dated November 13, 1940, telling of his plea for a delay in the strike: "Matles, pointing out that the industry was one in which the government was deeply interested, urged that the United States Conciliation Service be given an opportunity to try to effect settlement." And there was no strike. Not until June 22, 1941, when Germany attacked Russia, did the Communists in this country call for aggressive action against the Nazis; throughout the war, up to that time, the Communist Party, USA, had opposed our assistance to the western Allies in Europe; so, if munitions expert Small's thesis was accurate, the UE, supposedly a Communist-dominated union, should have been pulling strikes all over the place to assist their Red brothers overseas. Matles produced another clipping, this one from *The New York Times,* dated June 12, 1941, relating that of the strikes called against industries holding War Department contracts since the previous January 1, *not one* was called by the UE—of the 2,370,716 man-days lost in labor disputes in war industry, the UE was responsible for none.

Furthermore, said Matles, gathering steam, since the FBI or some other security department of the government investigates every person who works in a "sensitive" plant, it seemed very strange—*if* the UE was Communist-dominated—that after the government had done "all of the investigating and all of the checking and all of the clearing for sixteen years, there has not been a single officer or member of this union found to be guilty of a crime in violation of the laws having to do with the security of the United States. Not one. Not only has there been no one found guilty, but there has not been anyone indicted or even tried."

Humphrey was left remarkably speechless. At first all he could reply was, "I see." Then, gathering his cracked and dented armor about him, he retreated to wobbly questions about the UE's support of Wallace in 1948. Matles had clearly swept the field, and, considering the lack of any concrete evidence or lack of even any heavy suspicions raised against the patriotism of this union, which Humphrey had believed to be the most vulnerable of all and on which he had gambled the success of his entire hearings, considering all that, the UE seemed justified in issuing the statement: "Had the members of this union declared that war profiteering is fine, we would not be here today. . . . If our members had put their stamp of approval on the tax-price-wage squeeze that is wrecking the country's living standards, we would not be charged with endangering the country's security. . . . Had we called for atomic war, for $60 billion arms budgets, for distributing America's wealth to corrupt dictators like Franco and Chiang Kai-shek, we would not be under attack here."

Nothing about the hearings burnished Humphrey's reputation. His most honorable and admirable part in the whole proceedings was, when he saw that he had embarked on a blind and foolish venture, to end it all as quietly as possible. Holding the hearings at that overripe moment in history when McCarthyism had polluted politics was an irresponsible act, at best. But the UE was inaccurate when it accused Humphrey of McCarthyism. In the first place, he was sincere in his fear of what he time and again during the hearings identified as an operating, global Communist "apparatus." Believing this, and believing also that there were people in important places in American labor only too willing to be a part of the "apparatus," he pushed his fears the next logical step, to outline the dilemma which he insisted motivated the hearings: "Political views alone are one thing. Political views which lead to a particular type of political action is another thing. Political views held by people who discuss those views and act upon them in terms of voting, is one thing; but political views that are held by people who use them for purpose of espionage, for purposes of passing along vital information, is yet another thing. We in the free world, those of us who believe in democracy, have a terrible dilemma facing us—the sometimes divergent needs of civil rights and security precautions. Does the government of the United States have a right to protect itself from conspiratorial activity? Now, what do we do about this particular problem? In other words, the normal procedures which have been used on the basis of normal activity of people, political activity, seem not to apply. This is the problem that the free world faces, the problem that freemen face."

It was simple, straightforward jitteriness. Back home in Hennepin County, there were plenty of middle-class people who saw Reds coming up the bathtub drain and hiding behind the shower curtain—and Humphrey was always a middle-class Hennepinian. He would never have smeared decent union men, as McCarthy did, just for a political following. Not *just* for that. And Humphrey would never have done it without allowing himself first to be convinced that he was justified in the smear.

The only flaw in his investigation of Communists in labor unions was a fatal one—not once, not even indirectly, did he produce evidence of "conspiratorial activity." The answer to his question about whether or not the government has the right to protect itself from such things is, of course, one of the standard questions of government operations, and the answer is conceded to be "yes." Had Humphrey developed evidence of even one underfed conspiracy he would have been home safe with his integrity.

But he didn't.

In economic matters Humphrey almost always voted in a way that made the Americans for Democratic Action proud; it was not really hard to do, since most of the votes were on warmed-over New Deal programs. But in matters of subtle liberties, Humphrey held back, retrenched, and sometimes he even fought them, although he never did this publicly. In the mid-1950s the student affiliate of the ADA took its own independent stand that teachers belonging to the Communist party should be allowed to teach in public schools, should be judged as individuals rather than as members of any group and should be disciplined only if they performed badly in the classroom. Humphrey privately threatened to resign if the parent group did not try to force the students to rescind their stand. But even more eloquent was his public silence in regard to the Smith Act.

The Smith Act of 1940, aimed at wiping out or driving underground the strong radicalism that had cropped up in this country during the depression years, was broadly aimed, on sloppy legalisms, at people "who advocate the violent overthrow of the government." It was sold to the Congress on the grounds that it would combat Communism, and so it did; but it also made life rough on the Communists' (Stalinists') blood enemies, the Trotskyites, of whom some of Minnesota's best eventually wound up in prison under the Smith Act; and it also inhibited the hell out of just plain nonconformists. The ADA did not approve of the Smith Act; to the ADA it was repressive of freedoms. Humphrey did not agree with the ADA, of which he was a founder; during these hearings he engaged in this revealing exchange with Matles (note the shrewd meandering before the admission of where he stands on the Act; it is the kind of maneuvering that has somehow given him safe passage through both camps):

MATLES: . . . but I believe that you have stated you are, or at least one of the organizations you are associated with is, for the repeal of the Smith Act. There are some men serving jail sentences now because they said they were Communists.

HUMPHREY: That is not why they are serving jail sentences.

MATLES: Why are they?

HUMPHREY: They are serving jail sentences because the court determined that there was clear evidence that they were conspiring to overthrow the government.

MATLES: No; they didn't say that. Otherwise, your organization would not be for the repeal of the Smith Act.

HUMPHREY: They are teaching the overthrow of our government.

MATLES: I believe that your organization is for the repeal of the Smith Act.

HUMPHREY: I gather you are speaking of the Americans for Democratic Action?

MATLES: Yes; one of your organizations.

HUMPHREY: I don't recall that I ever voted on that particular provision. I never voted for its repeal.

MATLES: You have not?

HUMPHREY: No, sir.

MATLES: I am just saying that, if you haven't, I think you should, sir.

HUMPHREY: I have not.

MATLES: I made a mistake. I told some of your constituents in Minnesota that you have been advocating its repeal.

RUSS NIXON (another UE official): But, Senator, you are vice chairman of the ADA, and they announced that they were fighting for the repeal of the Smith Act and the McCarran Act. I was hoping you would get into that fight.

HUMPHREY: I have had a lot of fights.

NIXON: I know you have, and I hope you get into that one. (Humphrey did not respond.)

In the eyes of *all* liberals—the exceptions certainly would be so few as to justify this generalization—the most revolting act of Humphrey's political career occurred in 1954 when he sponsored the Communist Control Act, outlawing the Communist Party. Yet almost forgotten, and for some reason never given much importance by liberals, was the part he played in amending the McCarran Act of 1950 to set up concentration camps during wartime. (Six of these camps were constructed, but never put to use.) Actually it was an amendment that attempted in a clumsy way to make McCarran's

Stone Age legislation a little less brutal; in this Humphrey can mainly be faulted for the bad judgment of participating in the McCarran follies at all and of trying to pretty up a bad thing when he should have been spending his energies destroying it. But his action in 1954 was of a different quality. It was, if not perverse, at least hysterical.

There were, as there usually are for Humphrey—however irritating it may be to bring them into discussion—mitigating circumstances. For him, 1954, the year in which he sought his first reelection, was made especially burdensome by the avalanche of Republican charges that the Democrats were soft on Communism. Nixon was raging about the country displaying his talents for what Adlai Stevenson called "McCarthyism in a white collar." On a western tour the vice president repeatedly charged that liberal Democratic Senate candidates were "almost without exception members of the Democratic party's left-wing clique which ... has tolerated the Communist conspiracy in the United States."

Unless one can fix on a better reason among the bad reasons available, it almost seems likely that it was this tour of Nixon's which launched Humphrey into his wild effort to out-anti-Communist all anti-Communists. Humphrey knew that Nixon would eventually pass through his home territory and perhaps he wanted to put something into the record that would undercut anything Nixon said. If that was his purpose, he certainly succeeded.

However, the reason cannot definitely be assigned to any emotion or logic quite that precipitous. For some time Humphrey had been rattled by the anti-Communist fury then at its height in what was known for good reason as the McCarthy Period (the period was about to become so unbearable it would crest that very year with the censuring of McCarthy). He thought he had certainly earned his anti-Red bona fides with his own intraparty propaganda clashes in Minnesota, and yet here he was, six years later, still on the defensive about whether or not he loved Communists. He was known as a liberal Democrat in a reactionary period, and this made him suspect as at least a Communist dupe. Pique was the softest emotion that Humphrey felt under the circumstances. Speaking in Chicago in April of 1954 he had complained bitterly of being tied up in this defensive posture. The ADA and he, said Humphrey, had fought Communism "long before a junior Senator from Wisconsin found his way in Wheeling, West Virginia [where McCarthy had first leaped to headline stature by saying that he had in his possession a long list of Communists who worked in the State Department]. We are compelled to spend so much time challenging the big lie, that we seem to have little chance to search for the basic truths that might help lead mankind out of the present world impasse. Worst of all, at an hour when we should be exalting the institutions of freedom, we are allowing them to be tarnished by this madness of know-nothingness. . . ."

Someday a Ph.D. candidate with nothing better to do will add up all the congressional hours of defensive speech-writing and defensive speech-making and hours of sitting in dull fright at the thought of speaking out for the depressed people of this country and elsewhere, lest one be thought a revolutionary or soft on Communism, and the total will be impressive enough to support Humphrey's complaint. Fright and political paranoia made those years one of the most sterile eras in Congressional history.

And then came the campaign itself, overripe with the same kind of stupidity, and Humphrey decided he had had enough of it. (For one thing, H. L. Hunt, the Texas billionaire right-winger, had dispatched some of his hired slanderers to Minnesota. Later Humphrey was to say that if he thought he would ever have to go through such a dirty campaign again, he would drop out of politics. He did not get sympathy from everyone. Some of the radicals who had suffered from comparable attacks by Humphrey expressed delight at seeing him "get some of his own back.")

On August 12, when the Senate was considering the Butler bill to strengthen existing laws against Communist-dominated labor unions, Humphrey was moved, as he put it, to "give the back-row Red-hunters on the other side some real legislation to chew on." Remembering a bill to outlaw the Communist Party which had been introduced sometime previously by Senator Mike Mansfield, Humphrey put the idea to Mansfield, John Kennedy, and Wayne Morse that they revive the Mansfield bill and attach it to the Butler bill as an amendment. They agreed. Humphrey then put the idea to Lyndon Johnson, the Democratic leader, and he was overjoyed with the idea, but counseled that the support for the bill be made to look more conservative than the Humphrey, Morse, Kennedy authorship implied. Get Texas Senator Price Daniel, a horse-and-buggy mentality, to support it, too, Johnson advised. With Daniel among the authors, the bill was obviously certified for all conservative Democrats, and they flocked to it. Thus prepared, Humphrey went to the floor.

And there he began toying with the bigger fool on this issue, Eisenhower. In his State of the Union message, Ike had muttered something to the effect that "the subversive character of the Communist Party in the United States has been clearly demonstrated in many ways, including court proceedings. We should recognize by law a fact that is plain to all thoughtful citizens—that are dealing here with actions akin to treason—that when a citizen knowingly participates in the Communist conspiracy he no longer holds allegiance to the United States."

All right, said Humphrey, let us support our great President by carrying into law his anxiety on this point. In the Humphrey amendment's words, "The Congress hereby finds and declares that the Communist Party of the United States, although purportedly a political party, is in fact an instrumentality of a conspiracy to overthrow the government of the United States." Just what Ike had said. Under Humphrey's amendment, simple membership in the party would itself constitute an overt act aimed at overthrowing the government. He denied that outlawing the party would drive it underground, although he must have known that it would (J. Edgar Hoover had assured him that it would), and in later years he admitted this awareness when he said that Batista had driven the party underground in Cuba by outlawing it.

Humphrey declared, "I am tired of having people play the Communist issue. I want to come to grips with the Communist issue. I want Senators to stand up and to answer whether they are for the Communist Party or against it." It was time, he said, that the Senate stop handling bills year after year that dodged the issue, that it was time to put the burden on the Department of Justice and on the Subversive Activities Control Board, to find the Communists and to prosecute them.

Humphrey's ploy passed the Senate 84–0 the first time around, although the Republicans were privately furious because they felt that the amendment destroyed the Communist registration section of the Internal Security Act and muddied the Smith Act for prosecuting those advocating overthrow of the government; after all, one could hardly prosecute Communists for not registering, as previous laws required, if doing so constituted self-incrimination under Humphrey's Communist Control Act.

The House softened Humphrey's legislation, but when the softer side came back Humphrey successfully rehardened it, by a vote of 79 to 1. Only Estes Kefauver, the one gut fighter among Senate liberals in that era, voted against it. Then it went to conference committee, and when the most controversial of all the antisubversive laws of the 1940's and 1950's emerged from that august council it no longer identified the Communist Party as a criminal organization but did leave everything in a muddleheaded patchwork of phraseology. It made members of the Communist Party "subject to all the provisions and penalties of the Internal Security Act of 1950"; few could agree exactly what that meant. It was a hodgepodge, with thirteen elaborate criteria for deciding who was a member of the party. It also brought into existence Humphrey's threat of 1952, made during his investigation of Communist infiltration of unions, to prohibit members of Communist organizations from representing either side in a National Labor Relations Board proceeding. Perhaps the most confusing, and certainly the most dangerous, part of the act was that it not only pulled Communist organizations under the Internal Security Act but also fingered "Communist-infiltrated organizations"—which made it a wide-open game. One of the definitions of a Communist-infiltrated organization was "giving aid or support to a Communist foreign government" (like Yugoslavia? or Poland?). The law has never been successfully used.

Congressional opponents of the Humphrey concoction said it smelled like "week end beer" and that it was unconstitutional—an estimate that was concurred in outside Congress by the American Civil Liberties Union, Americans for Democratic Action, the Friends Committee, and the National Association for the Advancement of Colored People, among others on the left.

But it put Humphrey squarely on the side of the American Legion and the U.S. Chamber of Commerce. He and his co-conspirators were proud of how they had taken the play away from the Republicans. Said Walter George of Georgia, by that time one of Humphrey's greatest admirers (he campaigned for Humphrey), "They [the Republicans] brought in a political bill, so we just put a little more politics into it."

As for Humphrey, he must have felt considerable satisfaction, in a purely selfish way, when exactly one month and one day after final passage of his Communist Control Act, Vice President Nixon stopped over in his old hometown, Huron, South Dakota, to say, "We're kicking the Communists and fellow travelers and security risks out of government by the thousands." It was a bit of hokum which the homefolks must have thought sounded pretty pallid up beside what their Hubert had just accomplished.

Understandable as it was, in terms of political counter-gimmickry, Humphrey's anti-Communism on this occasion was as ruthlessly injurious to liberalism as anything he ever did. It only deepened the know-nothingness murk of which he had previously complained. It split the liberal ranks in dismay and embarrassment just when they were badly in need of cohesiveness. Around the country, liberals under attack from the right wing felt themselves to have been bludgeoned from behind by one of their trusted generals. Most members of the ADA were aghast at what their old colleague had done. Joseph Rauh, Washington attorney and a close friend of Humphrey, recalls: "I was in Europe in '54. When I came back I just couldn't believe what had happened. [Max] Kampelman had written the thing for him. Kampelman was the architect and sold it to Hubert as a superpolitical ploy. No question Humphrey was trying to defend it on that ground, that's right. Certainly the ADA attacked it. [Arthur] Schlesinger was acting chairman. As a matter of fact, at a CIO meeting in San Francisco later that year they got in a brawl, Kampelman tried to defend it to the CIO lawyers and we all let him have it. But they were trying to defend it on political grounds."

Humphrey was still playing politics when the McCarthy censure came before the Senate. In this trial of one of the most disastrous hacks to operate in the Senate since World War II, Humphrey opened his mouth only once, and then only to ask for a ruling on a point of procedure. But, then, to quote Rauh, "Where were the brave men of the Senate in 1954! Boy, you go look for them!" It is a good point, but it does overlook the fact that Humphrey's action earlier in the year had helped sear the ground for any buds of bravery that might have been sprouting.

Joining The Establishment

Though his freshness did not last long, Humphrey was at first a bright new sound in the Senate. When he sought to undo Harry Byrd's bogus economy committee, grandiloquently titled the Joint Committee on the Reduction of Nonessential Federal Expenditures, Humphrey did not pretend that he was embarking upon a polite fight. He used bold, rough language, for which he was temporarily shunned by the Senate Establishment, who walked out when he began to talk. It did not at first trouble him. Undiplomatically he remarked on March 2, 1950, "I have learned much today. I have learned that when one attacks the old-guard coalition in the Senate, through one of its prominent spokesmen, a freshman Senator is going to learn something. I have watched the rallying of the old-guard coalition on the floor of the Senate and I know why it happened." It had coalesced, he said, because he supported the Truman Administration 98 percent of the time while Byrd supported Truman no more than 36 percent of the time—not even so much as some Republicans—and Byrd did not want, nor did others of the old guard want, that sort of thing pointed out publicly on the floor.

Then Humphrey proceeded to deflate Byrd's claims, of which the most dramatic was his boast that in 1943 his economy committee had saved $38,000,000 by persuading the Roosevelt Administration to abolish the Civilian Conservation Corps, with forced reductions in the NYA and Works

Project Administration bringing other savings. This, Humphrey pointed out with considerable sarcasm, was nothing but a dream. Long before Byrd ever thought of proposing these reductions, Roosevelt had in his 1943 budget message asked Congress to slash nondefense spending because of the war and had, of course, fingered the carry-over Depression era programs as the most suitable to cut.

How cheering it was to hear the old frauds around the Senate being called old frauds. But Humphrey soon stopped doing it. Lyndon Johnson became his workaday hero, and Lyndon Johnson told him to go easy, to go along—and he would get along. Humphrey took the advice. By 1954 Walter George, the mandarin Democrat from Georgia, was telling Minnesota voters that it would be a "disaster" if they did not reelect Humphrey because in his first term he had become more and more "constructive and conservative." He had toned down most of his crusades, including especially the one for civil rights. "It's no great service to the party to be stubborn and dogmatic in one's views," he said in 1954. "The old New Dealer's sole idea was to get it done and the devil take the methods. Today, liberals are more concerned with protecting procedural rights and the use of proper Constitutional methods."

In 1958 William V. Shannon, then chief of the Washington bureau of the *New York Post,* wrote of the Humphrey-Johnson relationship: "From the moment he took office as leader of the minority Democrats in the Senate of 1953–54, Johnson was in search of a politician in the northern wing of his party with whom he could do business. The necessary qualifications were two. The man Johnson sought would have to be authentically representative of the liberal northern group and not a straddler or a modern doughface; he would have to stand ideologically at the core of his faction much as Senator Richard Russell of Georgia typifies the southern bloc. Secondly, he would have to be wholly a political man, ambitious, industrious, and fully engaged in his work; no 'dinner party Senator' or easy-going hack would suffice for the kind of serious partnership Johnson had in mind." Since only Humphrey fitted the prescription, "Johnson's cultivation of Humphrey was unflagging. If a private talk seemed desirable, Johnson usually went to Humphrey's office rather than have the latter come to him." The friendship finally reached that cozy point at which, as one southern senator describes it today, "they became big drinking buddies, often sitting up and drinking 'till 2 a.m. Bobby [Baker] was sometimes in there with them. I would give a pretty penny to know what deals they were hatching." The hooks went into Humphrey's fatty tissue, but they were received willingly. Humphrey became a Johnsonphile, not solely as a sycophant but as a man with his own ambitions.

When Joseph Clark of Pennsylvania first went to the U.S. Senate in 1957, he was informed by Humphrey that "Lyndon Johnson runs the Senate and will treat you well." Clark recounts this exchange on page two of his book *Congress: The Sapless Branch*—and he gives over much of the remaining 250 pages to detailing how in fact during the next four years Johnson destroyed every liberal effort either to pass progressive legislation or to reform the Senate, just as he had done in the preceding four years of his leadership. Along the way, Clark discovered how Humphrey had adjusted to the Establishment in such a way that he could, even while being gutted, convince himself that he was being treated well. In 1963, John Kennedy—realizing that some of his finance, international-policy, and welfare programs were going to get rough treatment in the conservative committees that would process them—gave his backing to Clark's crusade to have the size and the ratio of the Finance, Appropriations, and Foreign Relations committees expanded in such a way that several more liberal Senators could be slipped in to make the going easier. Then the leadership, including Humphrey, caved in; relying on Majority Secretary Bobby Baker's nose count, they said the fight was hopeless. Some Senate liberals used Baker as a kind of pope who would absolve them of their sins for not following their conscience.

Humphrey made use of Baker on numerous occasions in this way. Clark tells of another instance, when, in 1963, he proposed increasing the size of the Steering Committee from fifteen to nineteen to give it a semblance of ideological and geographical balance (southern conservatives still dominated it, and through it controlled all committee assignments). "To my chagrin and surprise," writes Clark, "Mansfield opposed my motion and Humphrey failed to support it. They told me later Bobby Baker had told them the votes were not there to approve the increase. Had [they] supported me, I believe we would have won."

It is unclear what use Johnson was to Humphrey, since no major legislation bearing Humphrey's authorship emerged from the Senate until he had been there a decade or more, but it was quite clear what use Johnson was getting from Humphrey. He was Johnson's link with the liberals, most of whom could not overcome a deep and abiding distrust of Johnson. Writing in the Washington *Post* of July 8, 1956, Robert C. Albright noted: "Symbolic of the new attempt to bridge the North-South gap are recent appointments to the Senate Democratic Campaign Committee. As chairman of the group, Majority Leader Johnson named Senator George A. Smathers of Florida, first Southerner in years to head up the unit. At the same time, Johnson appointed a leading northern liberal, Senator Humphrey, to act as vice chairman."

Here was a unique combination: Gorgeous George Smathers —the darling of Florida's special interests who in 1950 had run the dirtiest campaign in the history of Dixie to take the seat of liberal Claude Pepper—and lovable Hubert.

"I'll take care of the conservatives, and Hubert will take care of the liberals," cracked Smathers, "and together we'll walk down the middle."

Northern liberals who protested walking anywhere with such Southerners and who proposed instead a new party alignment along geographical lines that would ignore the South, were scolded by Humphrey as "defeatist."

An echo of Smathers's arm-in-arm description of odd alliances in the Senate was heard the next year from the jolly Minnesotan himself, when a reporter asked Humphrey if a certain bill would pass. Humphrey replied: "Oh, yes. Lyndon will round up the doubtful and I'll round up the faithful, and we'll put it over."

To many liberal observers the troubling aspect of all this, however, was that very few liberal programs were being "put over" by the Humphrey-Johnson type of teamwork.

Not that the two didn't have their little love spats. Just before the opening of the 1957 session Johnson was sulking. Humphrey had joined with a coalition of mainly non-Congressional Democratic liberals to advocate a sixteen-point program of action for the Party and especially for the Democrats in Congress. Others in the coalition included Eleanor Roosevelt and Adlai Stevenson—but Johnson and his mentor Sam Rayburn, Speaker of the House, shunned the group, whom they considered to be meddlers in Congress's business. Actually Congress had had no visible liberal business for so long that this was the reason the coalition came into being— to see if it could not inspire the Democratic leadership to some kind of constructive effort. But Johnson resented it. And he resented Humphrey's being part of it. He passed the word to other members of the Senate Club that Humphrey was no longer a member in good standing. He was to be cold-shouldered.

Just before Congress opened, Humphrey (according to Drew Pearson, January 13, 1957) gave Johnson a call to discuss some routine affair and quickly noticed that he was getting unusually brusque responses.

"What's the matter with you?" asked Humphrey. "You waging a cold war?"

"You broke faith with me," Johnson grumped.

"Now, Lyndon," Humphrey said, stroking the majority leader with his voice, "you know I wouldn't do that. You can get more votes out of this body than anyone else. You are a good leader, Lyndon. You are a great, great leader, Lyndon. I was simply trying to make you an even better leader." After a little more of that the two had made up, and the Senate Democrats under Johnson racked up a do-nothing year, with Humphrey, for the most part, going along.

Humphrey's reorganization retreat that Clark complained of in 1963 was not the first time he had deserted reformers to stick with the Establishment. In 1960, at the first Democratic caucus, Senator Albert Gore of Tennessee proposed that the membership of the Democratic Policy Committee be enlarged and that it be elected by all the Democrats rather than picked by Johnson. That was a year in which Johnson was going to make an all-out bid for the presidential nomination and he didn't want to offend any members, so he agreed to the change. "Excellent," Gore responded, "we'll settle the matter right now."

At that point Humphrey leaped up and disagreed. No, no, that was no way to do it, he said. "This is a very serious decision, a matter which we should think about and debate and decide with due caution. It should take a lot of thought. Now, let's sleep on it and come back and make our decision later." Delay was all that Johnson needed. When the Democrats met again, Gore's proposal was snowed under, and Humphrey had saved his leader.

It was perhaps because of these alliances which throughout the 1950's were offensive to most liberals that Mrs. Roosevelt changed her mind. In December, 1958, she said that of all the presidential candidates, Humphrey came closest to having the "spark of greatness" needed in the White House. But then she began to appraise his actions more closely, and one year later, in December, 1959, Mrs. Roosevelt said she had decided she would not work for Humphrey. She edged away gracefully, saying there were "just too many choices."

Humphrey developed a reputation as a brash liberal because he was articulate and eager to introduce a bill to advance almost any good cause. His first Senate speech on March 2, 1949, called for establishing a TVA-style authority to develop the Missouri River Valley. He has championed federal aid for housing, the arts, a variety of public facilities, a wilderness preservation system, mental health services, and practically anything else you can think of. Two education programs that he helped shape, the National Defense Education Act (NDEA) and federal aid to school districts heavily populated with federal government employees and defense-plant workers, pioneered in expanding federal aid to public schools. But both were dubious approaches because of (1) NDEA's science bias and (2) the incomes of government and defense workers are adequate enough to help finance their own community schools without a special subsidy that could be better spent in poor school districts.

Aside from his work for civil rights, Humphrey championed only one fundamental reform that promised to truly advance social justice—tax reform. In 1950 and 1951 he crusaded in a hostile Senate for amendments to plug giant loopholes in the federal tax laws that benefit only the wealthy, including LBJ's Texas favorite, the oil depletion allowance. "The federal tax laws are rigged against the middle- and low-income families—and for the big corporations," Humphrey observed in 1960. That, however, was the last year he was heard to speak out on behalf of the smaller taxpayers. His more recent pronouncements have been for toleration of corporate tax defenses.

Humphrey, like most politicians, has tried to peddle some legislation that would be banned if the truth-in-labeling bill applied to Congress. With his family drugstore in mind, he advocated "fair trade" or "quality stabilization" legislation, which would have given retailers a federal gun with which to rob consumers. Humphrey's bills would have outlawed many discount store bargains by permitting manufacturers to set prices on brand goods in interstate commerce and by compelling all retailers to conform to them. With such federal legislation, which Congress wisely has shunned, Humphrey hoped to overturn state court rulings that fair-trade laws are unconstitutional because they amount to nothing more than price fixing. And with a bow to his dairy-farming constituents in Minnesota, he opposed bills to make cheaper margarine available to housewives.

In 1963 a dozen liberal Senators fought one of the greatest giveaways in American history: the Communications Satellite Act that in effect turned the taxpayers' enormous investment in space research over to private industry for exploitation. Humphrey wasn't among the lonely band of liberals opposing it. In fact, he was a leader in working for the Act's passage.

His persistent advocacy of higher farm price supports, which made Humphrey appear to be the defender of the hallowed family farm, indicates how his brand of bread-and-butter liberalism often clings to outmoded New Deal programs while ignoring more significant lessons of the 1930's. For example, in 1954 Humphrey persuaded the Senate in a 45–44 vote to adopt an amendment that prevented Republican Secretary of Agriculture Benson from limiting the terms of members of county agricultural stabilization and conservation committees, who in effect determine which farmers will benefit by federal largesse. Benson wanted to limit the members to three consecutive terms because he believed the committees had become closed corporations. A decade later, the wisdom of Benson's proposal became apparent in a way that neither he nor Humphrey foresaw—domination of the county committees by white Southerners is forcing Negro farmers off the land partly because they can't get their fair share of federal farm aid or allotments. In the summer of 1964, a Humphrey amendment also killed antipoverty grants to poor farmers, substituting loans instead—which proved to be of little value to the poorest farmers who have no credit to qualify with or money to repay the loans.

The truth is that price supports chiefly benefit the two million larger, highly mechanized farming units (including the 2,000 elite farms in Humphrey's Minnesota), which account for about 85 percent of our agricultural production. Although 56 percent of the farmers are small and marginal operators, they receive less than 7 percent of the federal farm aid. "Major farm legislation directed at commercial farms has been successful in helping farmers adjust supply to demand, but it has not helped farmers whose production is very small," observed President Johnson's National Advisory Commission on Rural Poverty in 1967. Instead of raising the low incomes of rural residents, such legislation has helped "to create wealthy land-owners while largely bypassing the rural poor. . . . Any conceivable price policy for commercial agriculture, within the range of acceptability to the American taxpayers, would contribute very little to solving the poverty problem in rural America."

Humphrey's proposal for higher price supports tied to rigid production controls will freeze the capital-hungry farmers in relative poverty while at the same time forcing urban consumers to pay higher food prices.

"America is caught in the Urbanization Trap in the last third of the twentieth century," he said in a 1967 speech. "Seventy percent of us already live on 1 percent of the land," he observed, echoing the favorite theme of his old college debating partner, Secretary of Agriculture Orville L. Freeman. "We are going to have another 100 million Americans by the end of this century, and *all* of them will live in the cities if present trends continue. Our cities are starved for space, fresh air, recreation; our rural areas are starved for jobs and opportunity." But despite his long-time identification with the farm problem, he has never proposed a comprehensive program to reverse the powerful trend toward a society dominated by metropolitan anthills. He was unable during the 1960 presidential primary to propose any significant solutions to the woes of West Virginia (the second most rural state although it ranks fiftieth in farm production).

Many Americans have been forced into sprawling cities against their will in order to survive or to find decent-paying jobs. A 1966 Gallup Poll, for example, found that nearly half of the persons surveyed say they would prefer to live in a small town or on a farm. The views of twenty-one to twenty-nine-year-olds differ little from older persons, which indicates that distaste for metropolitan living isn't sentimental longing for a rural past. How free is a society that denies many of its citizens the opportunity to live as they would prefer—in small towns or rural areas—while uncontrolled economic forces create monstrous metropolitan areas that are becoming self-destructive?

Humphrey's humanitarian instincts tell him there is something profoundly wrong with a society that, in worship of mobility, denies half or more of its citizens any real option in choosing where they live. If he were living in a city slum, Humphrey said in 1966, he might "lead a mighty good revolt" himself—a remark which enraged reactionaries and which, the following day, Humphrey toned down considerably. "Thirty-five million Americans still live in poverty; slum schools still turn out children who can't read the labels on a medicine bottle; many of the children in the Head Start program identify the teddy bear on the chart as a rat," Humphrey also observed in 1966. He sounds like he's all heart.

He is aware of how rural migration only complicates attempts to eliminate metropolitan poverty. He talks of the big city's "pressure-cooker atmosphere," piling up the population in coastal megalopolises while draining America's heartland of people; the fact that half of the people now working on farms won't be needed in the future; the need for creating more and better jobs for the poor. The old Humphrey itch for new federal programs to solve whatever ails you still occasionally surfaces—and gets him into trouble with LBJ. At a 1967 cities-of-tomorrow symposium in Washington, Humphrey revived the idea of federal aid to stimulate construction of new towns. But he sensed the futility of making the proposal by observing that he might get into trouble for daring to suggest another new program.

Perhaps the underlying reason for the timidity of Humphrey liberalism is its self-defensive worship of private enterprise—the failure of the liberal vision to see beyond the either-ors of capitalism and socialism, a heritage of the Great Depression and Cold War emotionalism. Humphrey assumes that government and industry working together can build paradise by a kind of spontaneous combustion. In a 1967 speech, for example, he talked of government financing needed public facilities in rural areas which he said will have to take the initiative in attracting industry—a suggestion that is somewhat like advising an unemployed slum youth to save his money so he can get ahead. The small towns and cities in rural areas have already done everything but deed over their streets and homes to bribe industry into creating jobs.

The long years of waiting for a Social Security-tied medical assistance program have been the result of the expert and heavily financed lobbying opposition on the part of the American Medical Association; but the liberals, for their part, cannot claim to have been especially vigorous in meeting the opposition until the 1960's. In 1935, Roosevelt told Congress, "I am not at this time recommending the adoption of so-called 'health insurance,'" but the manner in which he pushed through his Social Security Act that year left many in Congress with the understanding that he would shortly be back to tie medical assistance to it. He did not, however, make any effort to do so in the remaining decade of his Administration, although in 1944 and again in 1945 he talked in vague terms about "the right to adequate medical care." When President Truman took office after Roosevelt's death in 1945 he asked for enaction of a prepaid medical insurance plan for persons of all ages, supported by a raise in Social Security deductions. Stiff opposition within and without Congress was immediate and successful. Then, in 1949, it looked as if there might be a breakthrough; Truman had just upset the odds-on favorite, Dewey, and he had carried in with him enough Democrats to control both Houses.

That was Humphrey's first year. He is fond of saying these days, and does say on every appropriate occasion, that the first bill he introduced after arriving in Washington was for medicare.

What he does not add is that, to everyone's surprise, late in November he announced his agreement with Senator Paul

Douglas, another whom liberals depended on, that while he believed in the "principle" of Social Security health insurance, he recognized the "practical difficulties of a nationwide program of health insurance" and he said that Congress should work out the "problems of administration" through "further research, further hearings" before they reach "the legislative action stage." He favored the six preliminary points in the Truman health bill but would prefer that the seventh, the compulsory insurance point (really the guts of the plan), go over to the next session. He said it would be better to avoid a showdown on point seven until Truman got a mandate from the voters—which, of course, everyone thought he had indeed received by his election in 1948.

So no action was taken, and the measure went over until the next session, and then over to the next, and so on until, sixteen years later, it was apparently safe to enter what Humphrey had called the "legislative action stage."

While it is true that Humphrey used to always call himself a liberal, he usually ducks it these days, preferring something more general, like, "I'm still in the mainstream of political progressivism." In civil rights affairs he cannot, because of his caution and his erraticism, be considered as more than an eager moderate. In economic matters, he was an updated New Dealer, no more (and in saying this one must realize just whom we are placing Humphrey with; John Rankin, the unspeakable Congressman from Mississippi, was, after all, the father of the REA in the House, and no one in the Senate was more faithful to the New Deal program than Mississippi's other gift to the Dark Ages, Theodore Bilbo).

During his years in the Senate Humphrey usually scored 100 percent with the Americans for Democratic Action for his voting record and he never fell below 97 percent; but one does not need to be very radical to score high with the ADA. In 1950, except for two Negro issue votes, Lister Hill of Alabama was rated as high as Humphrey by the ADA. The next year both Hill and the other Alabamian, John Sparkman (who calls himself, and is, a moderate conservative), were rated perfect, along with Humphrey; and this was true again in 1953. In 1957 and 1958 Stuart Symington, rarely less than a global hawk and a moderate conservative in economic affairs, was rated perfect, and he had missed it by only one vote in 1954. Carl Hayden of Arizona, who has never had the reputation of being exactly a bomb thrower, was rated perfect in 1948, came within one vote of being rated as high as Humphrey (perfect) in 1954, and in 1956 he came within two votes. With all due respect to whatever courage it took to be civilized in the United States Senate during the 1950's, one must bear in mind that such rating scales as that of the ADA measured no more than a kind of surface civility.

The fault does not lie with the measuring stick. It is just that the material with which the Senate customarily works leaves a man little room for extending his liberalism, or for showing his willingness to do so. In any event, whether from that cause or, more likely, because he simply did not want to differ from them materially, Humphrey went into the 1960 presidential campaign with no dramatically unique coloration compared to that of his rivals, Senators Johnson, Kennedy, and Symington. This, of course, was contrary to the impression he wished to leave. Early in the year he said, "Liberals are waiting for a leader—one who stands out from the rest. My job is to go to the convention keeping my flame alive." Considering his record, that flame was fed more by gas than by heavy fuel. Between 1953 and 1959, which is the span during which their Senate careers overlapped, Humphrey differed from Johnson, Kennedy, and Symington on only 42 of the 893 roll-call votes on which all four were counted. That is, he stood alone, without company from *any* of the others, only 42 times. Some of these were key issues; nearly a third of his lone-wolf votes were to reform tax laws, to plug loopholes that benefit special interests; he marched alone to defend the consumer against swindles, to keep the farmer supplied with peak government prices; he alone voted to abolish the antiquated electoral college and to establish

a national presidential primary and direct election of the
president. And only he, in 1959 (one of those ironic memories) voted to extend the draft by only two instead of four
years and to establish a commission to reform its inequities.
His lonely votes were always cast for the public good. Still,
when the sum was taken, he was discovered to have voted
no different from Symington on 89 percent of the roll-calls,
no different from Kennedy on 83 percent and no different
from Johnson on 79 percent. At best, Humphrey's flame flick-
ered between 10 to 20 percent higher, depending on whether
he was compared with a leading Midwest moderate or a
leading southern conservative. In a legislative body where
the margin of liberalism is so narrow, the chance to be a
standout liberal is rather slight and, on the whole, a rather
academic measure.

The ladder by which Humphrey climbed into the bosom of
the Senate Establishment was, true enough, constructed out
of myriad compromises of principles. But this, in a legislative
body in which virtually everyone is willing to compromise his
principles from time to time, is not enough to lift one onto a
special plateau. A much surer way is to possess some special
magic, black or otherwise, and this Humphrey has always had.
His bag contains an amazing immunity to soot, smudge, rumor
and guilt by association; he has a kind of built-in absolution
that is priceless to a politician. It extends in all directions.

Arthur Schlesinger Jr., plugging away for more tolerance
for his candidate, Robert Kennedy, recently wrote in exaspera-
tion: "It is more than a fact that Robert Kennedy at the age
of 27 served briefly as a junior counsel on the McCarthy committee. After all, Hubert Humphrey in the same period and
at a much older age (43) was teaming up with Martin Dies
to sponsor the Communist Control Act of 1954. Eugene
McCarthy voted to sustain every HUAC contempt citation
during his time in the House. . . . Yet Humphrey and
McCarthy are forgiven for acts committed well beyond the
age of discretion, while Kennedy's youthful offense keeps him

under a shadow. This is, I think, only because Humphrey and McCarthy do not fit into the prosecutor stereotypes." Schlesinger's professorial astonishment is much more understandable in regard to Humphrey because one's sins are usually judged proportionate to one's fame, and Humphrey has always been a much more important politician than McCarthy. Schlesinger's point is well made, and what is true of Humphrey's survival of certain deeds is also true of his survival of certain friendships. The burden of cronyship that figures so heavily in the lives of, say, Truman and Johnson has rested with angelic lightness on the round shoulders of Hubert Humphrey.

One of his closest friends is Freddie Gates (Humphrey once described him as his *very* best friend), who, until his alliance with Humphrey carried him to a higher social plateau, was best known around Minneapolis as a very big operator in pinball machines, penny arcades, and juke boxes; but then he gained, through Humphrey, credentials as vice chairman of the Minnesota Small Business Advisory Council and later as a member of the Post Office Advisory Committee. Their friendship was for a time material for grim jokes in Minnesota, but the snickering has mostly passed, perhaps because Gates has now moved up from pinballs to bowling alleys and Humphrey has carefully put it around that an FBI check several years ago cleared his friend of any suspicions of shadiness.

After his first session in Congress, Humphrey came back to Minnesota to spend the summer on the luxurious estate of Frank Griswold, owner of Griswold Signal Company of Minneapolis and other companies that had done well in war contracts. At the time Griswold was being besieged by the Internal Revenue Service over a little matter of $250,000 which the IRS said he owed the government. Orville Freeman was one of Griswold's attorneys. The case was dropped. There was some talk, of course, but not for long.

Humphrey's luck is still holding.

On May 24, 1966, three executives of the Anheuser-Busch Company and their wives, and the head of the brewery's public relations firm and his wife, contributed a total of $10,-

000 to the "President's Club." Four weeks later the Justice Department dropped an antitrust suit against Anheuser-Busch. Less than a month after the suit was dropped, the head of the Antitrust Division was flying off in an Anheuser-Busch plane to attend the All-Star game in St. Louis; host for the plane trip was A. A. Busch III, general manager of the brewery. There were some suspicious people who condemned the whole affair as pretty shoddy; some even intimated that the suit had been dropped in return for the contribution, and that the plane trip was a way of shaking hands on the deal. President Johnson was damned in Congress and in the press. Assistant Attorney General Donald F. Turner properly took some cuffs. But Vice President Humphrey came off with very little abuse, although *he* was the man who invited Turner to ride in the Busch plane and, in fact, it had been Humphrey who arranged the whole affair from the Washington end. Turner said he didn't know the Anheuser-Busch plane was to be used until the last minute and then, after hesitating only briefly, decided that he should follow Humphrey's lead.

Every time businessmen who use questionable tactics are mentioned in the same breath with Lyndon Johnson, most people automatically assume that Johnson is in league with them. With Humphrey, it's just the opposite, although it must be said that in recent months Humphrey's imperviousness to scandal has been sorely tested.

Late in 1967, Congressman H. R. Gross of Waterloo, Iowa, a member to whom many newsmen pay little attention because he seems to seek it so desperately, took the House microphone to declare some bad news that could not be ignored. He spoke of a "deal" between friends in government and in private industry that "reeks of incompetence or fraud, or both." It seems that Napco Industries of Minneapolis, owned by men who were close friends and campaign contributors of Humphrey and of that other august Minnesotan, Secretary of Agriculture Orville Freeman, had a gear factory in Detroit that was becoming a burden; so they sold it to a specially formed corporation in India, which got the $4,000,-000 to buy Napco's machinery et al. from the Agency for International Development. Later, government investigators discovered that much of the machinery which Napco shipped to India was in obsolete, irreparable condition. It looked an awful lot as if Humphrey's friends had unloaded some useless machinery on a jerry-built company in India.

In swinging this loan through AID—and it was, by the way, the first time AID had ever financed a deal for *used* machinery—Napco had the good services of, among others, Herbert J. Waters, an AID official who used to be Humphrey's administrative assistant, and Max Kampelman, who was for six years Humphrey's legislative counsel in the Senate and is still looked upon as his closest adviser and confidant. Kampelman is a Napco director and stockholder. Kampelman, of course, hotly denied exerting any political influence personally or through Humphrey. Newsmen were prevented from learning more about the transaction because the Justice Department took all records and put them off limits.

In January, 1968, Waters, who is still one of Humphrey's advisers on farm policies, resigned from AID. It was disclosed that he and five other AID employees had, as Felix Belair, Jr., of *The New York Times* delicately put it, "accepted gratuities" from an Antwerp contractor, "including favors from women" the contractor hired to visit the AID officials at various rendezvous spots around Europe. For his thoughtfulness, the Antwerp contractor was allowed to increase his AID contract price by $250,000.

And in between those two AID mishaps, Gross took the House floor to charge that the Government lost $3.1 million after Eugene P. Foley, one-time aide to Humphrey, approved a contract with Universal Fiberglass Corporation, a Minnesota company, to build three-wheel carts for the U.S. Post Office Department despite a warning from the General Services Administration that the firm had neither the finances nor the technical capacity to do the work. In 1966 the firm defaulted on its contract. The loan was processed by the Small Business

Administration, of which Foley was the top administrator. During the 1960 campaigns, Foley was an executive assistant to Humphrey. Congressman Gross charged that the firm's "powerful political friends in Washington" had swung the faulty loan, but he did not accuse Humphrey by name and the scandal did not stick to him.

Neal D. Peterson, one of Humphrey's aides, is the brother of Roger Peterson, Universal Fiberglass's attorney. Although Humphrey's office insisted that Neal Peterson quit trying to help Universal Fiberglass after Humphrey became vice president, Sanford Watzman, Washington correspondent for the Cleveland *Plain Dealer,* discovered records showing that fourteen long-distance calls were placed between the New York offices of Rand Development Corporation and Humphrey's offices between March, 1966, and March, 1967. Rand Development, which is based in Cleveland, owns Universal Fiberglass.

Watzman also discovered that George H. Bookbinder, vice president of Rand Development, was a fund-raiser for Humphrey in his bid for the presidential nomination in 1960. Watzman reported that Bookbinder played a "large role" in 1960, although Bookbinder insists that he raised no funds for Humphrey but only gave his own money.

Rand Development got another assist from a Humphrey friend when, in its December, 1966, and again in its January, 1967, issues, *Pageant* magazine ran featured articles about a vaccination developed by Rand which was being tried against cancer. Although the vaccine had passed no tests whatsoever and was way down in the experimental stage, the cover of the December *Pageant* heralded: "AT LAST! SCIENTISTS REPORT ANTI-CANCER VACCINE!" The vaccine did not cure cancer, of course, and as soon as the magazine appeared on the newsstands late in November the U.S. Food and Drug Administration sought an injunction against further manufacture of the vaccine.

Cancer victims weren't being helped by this publicity, but Rand Development Corporation was benefitting rather noticeably. Its stocks shot up. As District Judge James C. Connell noted, in his hearing on the injunction, "the stock went up every time [Rand] scientists had an interview with anybody who had anything to do with publications." In 1966 the Rand stock went up from $2 to $3 to $54.

Gerald A. Bartell, publisher of *Pageant*, is not only a friend of Humphrey but was his advisor on television matters in his 1960 campaign. Humphrey's office helped set up meetings between Rand and FDA.

The Universal Fiberglass three-wheel cart episode wasn't the first time Humphrey's name was linked to post office waste. In 1954, George Etzell, Republican national committeeman from Minnesota and publisher of the Clarissa *Independent*, attacked Humphrey for pushing through the Democratically-controlled post office committee and thence through Congress a bill authorizing the Postmaster General to contract for sending mail around New York City via pneumatic tubes. Etzell said the cost of the operation reached $1,000,000 a year before Postmaster Summerfield cancelled the contract and substituted two trucks for the tubes. Cost of the trucks: $25,000 a year. When asked about the million-dollar legislation, which had been passed only four years previously, Humphrey said he could "scarcely remember" it. But Etzell's exposé flopped. For some reason, Humphrey got mostly sympathy out of the attack.

Far more than most important politicians, Humphrey is the creature of his associates. There are some who contend—and some who do are quite close to Humphrey—that he was literally the creation of a group of intellectuals (graduate students and professors) at the University of Minnesota at a time when Minnesota politics was in surging flux and they saw an opportunity to move out of the academic and into the practical. Humphrey was one of them, but he was the glibbest and his glands were the most hyperactive, so he was selected as the vehicle for their experiment.

Of those who coached him and kept him spurred for the campaigns, as well as toning up his patriotic superthink, the most influential were Kampelman, who took a Ph.D. in political science from that university; Dr. Evron Kirkpatrick, one of Humphrey's teachers; and Arthur Naftalin, another Ph.D. in political science who became Humphrey's secretary when he was mayor of Minneapolis and who is himself mayor of that city, serving his second term. There are other names inseparably linked to Humphrey. But in the genesis and development of Humphreydom, none hold quite the same intimate association as Kampelman, Kirkpatrick, and Naftalin. Which makes it all the more remarkable that virtually none of the notoriety of Kampelman and Kirkpatrick (Naftalin has achieved no notoriety) has attached itself to Humphrey.

Aside from the unhappy AID business in which Kampelman participated, he was also one of the organizers of the D.C. National Bank in 1962, a bank whose beginnings (because of the politics behind it) gave off a slight aroma. Using Kampelman as his reference, Bobby Baker—*the* Bobby Baker, now under indictment for income tax evasion and larceny —was permitted to buy some of the first stock issue, and later he obtained an unsecured loan of $125,000 from the bank to purchase a house. Some of Baker's stock found its way into the hands of gambling characters in Nevada. After serving as Humphrey's legislative counsel for six years, Kampelman channeled most of his energies into the law firm of Strasser, Spiegelberg, Fried, Frank & Kampelman— a firm which, as you might expect, has little trouble getting lobbying jobs, all quite aboveboard, so far as any critics could tell, but some of the lobbying jobs certainly did take Kampelman into areas which might be considered foreign to one whose career was launched from the Humphrey office. That is, it was hired by the American Textile Manufacturers Institute in 1967 to watch out for "legislation with regard to flammable fabrics and consumer protection." When the American Textile Manufacturers Institute talks about consumer protection it does not mean exactly the same thing that Ralph Nader means. And the previous year Kampelman's firm had been hired by Wards Co., Inc., of Richmond, a retail firm, to lobby on laws affecting overtime pay.

Congressmen and the public began to look more closely at Humphrey's most intimate adviser late in 1967 when President Johnson considered him for chairman of the Washington, D.C., City Council. Actually, his appointment to something in the federal line had been anticipated since late in 1964 when the FBI began checking him out, but nothing materialized for another three years. Then Gross jumped on him for his AID ties, and Senator Carl T. Curtis of Nebraska had a few cutting remarks to make because Kampelman had been a conscientious objector during the war but had wangled a Marine Corps commission after the war, which he later resigned. And his various lobbying connections began to come out, so, not wishing Congress to probe into his affairs any deeper, Kampelman asked that his name be withdrawn from consideration.

Dr. Kirkpatrick added his splash of color to the Humphrey marquee in February, 1967, when *The Nation* magazine discovered that he had been supervising one of the CIA's conduits. That was the season of the big CIA stink, when it seemed that *no* activities in the country had been left untouched: labor unions, newspaper guilds, universities, magazines, student organizations—all had been tainted by CIA money, some of which was channeled through bogus foundations or real foundations which served as a front for the work. At that time Dr. Kirkpatrick had been for twelve years executive director of the American Political Science Association, a prestigious fraternity which has about 16,000 professors in its membership. For most of that same period he had been executive director of Operations and Policy Research, Inc., an organization established to help the United States Information Service, the government's propaganda arm, distribute more persuasive broadsides and magazines and books.

To do this work Kirkpatrick hired scores of professors across the country and doled out funds which were supplied to him not only by the USIA, but by the State Department and by the Pentagon—and by the CIA, coming through two front foundations, the Pappas Charitable Trust of Boston and the International Development Foundation, Inc. When this was disclosed, a minority group of professors in the American Political Science Association tried to get Kirkpatrick fired, but so great was the influence of government contracts within that organization that the movement was easily beaten back. Nor was Humphrey hurt by it. In fact, it was discovered at the same time that Humphrey had been getting draft deferments for CIA-supported officials of the National Student Association so that they could continue working for the government on the sly, and no outcry was heard because of this.

The influence wielded by these men does not reveal itself dramatically in Humphrey's views on domestic economic and social issues. But the influence of the group has been highly visible in Humphrey's rigid and sometimes brutal attitude toward all Communists and many radicals, both in this country and abroad. In the judgment of Joseph Rauh, "Humphrey has always had two camps from the day he got down here [Washington]. There were those people who wanted to make him into a conservative [on Communism, war, civil liberties]—Kampelman and [James] Rowe and the leaders of that operation—and there were those of us who wanted to keep him on our side [the liberal side]." Asked where Kirkpatrick fitted in Rauh said, "With Kampelman. Kirkpatrick and Kampelman and [Richard] Scammon (former director of the Census Bureau) were CIA agents. That's a public declaration, they were CIA agents. You don't know they had a foundation, the three of them? Kampelman is the operator, he's the boss of it. Kirkpatrick works for Kampelman. The three of them were the foundation that got the [CIA] money. That's the right-wing pressure on Hubert. Kampelman always wanted to make Hubert look like a conservative, still wants to make Hubert look like a conservative, and he's got Hubert looking like a conservative."

But if Humphrey is somehow miraculously protected from guilt, he does not try to hoard his powers but attempts to share them with his colleagues, and for this they, with good cause, love him.

As James P. Boyd, Senator Thomas J. Dodd's former assistant, has pointed out, the panel appointed by Humphrey to try Dodd—and especially the chairman of that panel, Senator John Stennis of Mississippi—were ideally selected for their willingness to protect the Senate establishment and to gloss over all of the charges that might lead significantly into the broad questions of senatorial conduct. All generic conflict of interest was set aside. Instead the panel zeroed in on the narrowest charges, the charges that could not lead the inquiry beyond the conduct of one man in one specific instance. It was this kind of cooperation that the rest of the Senate appreciates from Humphrey. *He* knew that it would just stir up needless trouble to put senatorial conduct on trial; the line might stretch over the heads of a hundred Senators, but with the Vice President's cooperation the only underwear hung out to dry would be Dodd's alone.

The two-volume records of the Dodd hearings, or trial, held in 1966 and 1967, are very instructive. In those records one finds so many prominent Senators listed as having committed some of the very same indiscretions that Dodd was charged with that had the Ethics Committee moved one degree from its anti-Dodd path, it could easily have opened a Pandora's box of embarrassment for the entire Senate establishment. If this had happened, one of the first to be forced into a blush would have been Hubert Humphrey, for the marks of his friendship for the principals in this shoddy case are found everywhere.

One of the charges against Dodd was that he had misused his senatorial office by going off to Europe on an errand meant to salvage the lobbying career of Julius Klein, a citizen of this country who had risen to prominence in Washington's shadow world as an influence peddler. He liked to be called "General," and in fact he was a two-star general, having been appointed such in the Illinois National Guard as a reward for his contributions to the Republicans. His election as National Commander of the Jewish War Veterans—from which pressure point he aided a number of his cronies in the Senate

—was abruptly reversed when the group discovered that he was a paid lobbyist for some ex-Nazi industrialists who were trying to get their impounded holdings returned to them.

His clients were mostly warmaking industrialists and right-wing politicians from West Germany, and at the height of his career he was supplied with $150,000 a year to keep Washington's politicians pliable to West German interests, as represented in the person of Chancellor Konrad Adenauer. Klein, like his clients, detested "soft-liners" and "appeasers" who tried to get along with the eastern bloc. He stood in direct opposition to the more flexible and the milder foreign policy that President Kennedy was trying to establish.

Until 1963 life was rosy for Julius Klein, who claimed to be a war hero, who claimed that he had "made" General MacArthur into a world figure through his own genius as a publicity expert, and who claimed the undying gratitude and friendship of most of Washington's powerful men. He was full of bluff and swagger. The pose was not altogether false. He did have powerful friends, and Hubert Humphrey was among them. Together, they hosted parties for some of Europe's more notorious militarists.

But in 1963 Senator William Fulbright held his investigation of foreign agents, and in that inquisition the career of Julius Klein was held up for a full public inspection. The sight was not pretty. Klein was portrayed as an overbearing, pushy, big-mouth pest whose entrance into the backrooms and barrooms of Washington drew groans from some of the occupants—contrary to the popular role he had cast himself in when dealing with his clients. When the report of the Fulbright investigation hit Germany, Klein's clientele began to fall away drastically. To save his career, he began to hound his Senate cronies (many of whom had received generous campaign contributions from him) into spreading it on thick so that the militarists and industrialists of West Germany would continue to retain him as their lobbyist. He especially wanted evidence and statements from other Senators to discredit Fulbright. In a microcosm, it was a contest between the Cold War supporters on the one hand and, on the other, those who hoped that this country could enter a new era of accommodation with the mellowing Communist bloc. To that end, Klein's greatest victories would be in seeming to carry "liberals" to his side. And he was quite successful. He solicited —and received—letters of comradely affection and advice not only from ultraconservatives like Karl Mundt and Bourke Hickenlooper, who could be expected to agree with Klein's foreign policy, but also from mild liberals like Abraham Ribicoff and Jacob Javits and Wayne Morse. He also got the closest of support from the Senate's chameleon, Everett Dirksen, who votes every way on every important subject but, in the long run, comes out on the side of reaction.

The evidence of friendship between Hubert Humphrey and this smudged influence huckster was hard for some liberals to accept, but here were the letters and the evidence spread on the record:

> . . . my dear friend Julius . . . I can't quite believe that it is necessary to give a personal testimony again and again as to our friendship and as to my respect for you. You have that in writing many times and you have the demonstration of such respect by many personal acts on my part. . . . Now, my dear friend Julius, let me dare to give some advice. You do not need to send any more letters to Senator Fulbright, nor does anyone else need to do so. The hearings on foreign agents and nondiplomatic representation are over. You came out very well, despite one or two news stories that may have caused you some embarrassment. You perform your duties well. You have many friends in this Congress. You have given outstanding service to your clients. You have nothing to apologize for and much to be proud of. With such a fine record, you have nothing to worry about. You are at liberty to show this letter to anyone you please, including the representatives of the German government.

That was on January 16, 1964. But it was not enough to satisfy Klein, who begged for another letter of praise, and on February 6, 1964, Humphrey wrote again:

> When you are speaking to some of your clients, I wish you would show them this letter. There is not a single thing in the reports of the Fulbright Committee that indicates that you have done anything improper. To the contrary, those reports reveal that you have done a very good job of representing your clients. Furthermore, those hearings and reports reveal that you have a host of friends in the Congress of the United States in both political parties, and men of considerable stature in the Congress who have a high regard for you and respect for your professional ability. Well, Julius, sometimes those who seek to get ahead do so at the expense of the reputation and the welfare of others. This seems to be what some people are trying to do to you and it is a nasty business. I am very sorry. My very best wishes to you. And I hope that things will turn for the better. Be assured of my continued friendship.

Since the man who wrote these fond assurances of support was at that time the Democratic Whip of the U.S. Senate, the second most powerful man in the majority of the upper house, it was the kind of sycophancy that was likely to impress the rulers of Germany. Naturally, when Klein sent Senator Dodd packing off to Germany to tout his career, he made sure to put in Dodd's briefcase instructions to read the above quote when talking with top German officials as well as this other bouquet from Humphrey (the Senate records do not show when this one was written):

> . . . Julius Klein has more friends in the Senate and the House of Representatives than any man I know. We respect his partisanship, but even more, we cherish his friendship. He is always welcome here, and I do appreciate his advice and counsel.

In Klein's covering letter of instructions to Dodd, he reminded the Connecticut Senator, "Chancellor Adenauer will always be grateful to you, the late Styles Bridges and Hubert Humphrey for your marvelous support and the various receptions you gave him when he and Dr. von Brentano were visiting Washington." Dodd and Bridges were two of the Senate's most notorious Cold Warriors of the fanatical anti-Communist phalanx; one is likely to be surprised at first to see HHH grouped with them, as a host for the old hawk Adenauer and his war-machine liaison, Dr. von Brentano; but the surprise will not last.

Before departing for Germany, Dodd was urged by Klein to "let Jack Javits brief you again; also Dirksen, Humphrey, Morse and Symington," so that he would have his recitation of Klein's splendors down perfectly. And when there was a slight delay in Dodd's travel plans and he could not fly off to Germany at the same time Klein was there, the latter wrote (February 24, 1964) in slight pique: "Had I known that your schedule would have kept you in Washington I would have asked either Senator Humphrey or Senator Symington to make a quick trip here on a week-end to speak on behalf of their Democratic colleagues just as Javits did for Dirksen and other of his Republican colleagues. Meanwhile, I am sure that you have seen the wonderful letter that Hubert Humphrey has sent to me."

Here were powerful ties, indeed, if Klein could expect Humphrey just to pop over for a weekend of hustling. It is not likely, actually, that Humphrey would have done it. He was far too busy putting together the Senate machine to push through the civil-rights legislation that he and Johnson would run on that year. If the anti-Communist side of Humphrey had to be momentarily sidetracked to accommodate his ambitions, however, it did not mean the civil-rights fight could eclipse the other entirely. He desperately needed every Senator he could muster to fill out the antifilibuster platoons, yet, for the sake of Klein's career and for the sake of the hard-line relationship Klein strengthened between the Pentagon

and the State Department in this country and the Adenauer-
ites in Germany, Humphrey gave his blessing to Dodd's
departure. Later, when critics began to question whether
Dodd's profession of support for civil rights could mean much
since he had flown to Europe at the peak of the Senate battle
in 1964, he produced a letter from Humphrey, written June
21, 1966, taking his side: "I did, indeed, assure you that your
brief absence would not injure our position" (in the civil-
rights debate). Instead of clearing Dodd, however, the letter
only succeeded in implicating Humphrey with Dodd's more
shiftless affairs. Humphrey felt the critics were unfair in this.
He sincerely held himself blameless. Civil rights are good,
but to him as always the fight against the international
Red menace is much more important, and had not Dodd
told him that he was going to Germany for the Senate Subcommittee on Internal Security to seek information about the
Red network?

The Politics
of Brotherhood

"People are people and as such they are entitled to respect,"
Humphrey once said, explaining his concept of civil rights. "I
learned that from my Daddy and Mommy." Filial sentiment
rather than Constitutional logic or philosophical egalitarian-
ism—*this* is one reason the Negro struggle for equality during
the last two decades has done a great deal more for Hubert
Humphrey than Hubert Humphrey has done for it. This is
said in full realization that he has from time to time shown
some ingenuity in furthering the cause. Like a good liberal,
he sometimes *spoke* in behalf of the Negro. He was fiery
when it improved his career, and he banked his fires when
this improved it further. He was a hard-line integrationist
when he needed headlines of that sort to get a national status,
and he was understanding of the white South when he was
intent upon building intraparty bridges to power in the
Senate. He, not Dirksen, who is sometimes credited with it,
oiled the passage of the civil-rights program of 1964 through
the Senate. But to be realistic it must be said that this took
something less than genius; the time was overripe to the point
of spoilage; the death of Kennedy had supplied the shock
needed to loosen the dead hand of Dixie on the Senate (at
least long enough for this legislation to be pushed through),

and Lyndon Johnson, who wanted it on his record for the 1964 campaign, was operating at the highest point of influence that he was to be blessed with in his presidency. Humphrey helped build the success, but he certainly was not the architect of it. And, after all, who of those Senators who had been at the very center of power for twenty years without moving the civil-rights iceberg would dare take much credit for something achieved in 1964—a decade after the Brown decision, sixteen years after President Truman and the Democrats had sworn in their platform (accompanied by Humphrey's somewhat self-serving trumpet call) to do something about segregation, three years and a dozen deaths and hundreds of bombings and beatings and jailings after the civil-rights movement began its dazzling attack on the southern establishment. What is Humphrey's role in the civil-rights fight, take it all in all? Rather slight.

Under Humphrey's mayoralty, Minneapolis became the first municipality with a Fair Employment Practice statute. It was a good one, specific, emphatic, and shored up with criminal penalties. For Minnesota, however, it was not a singular action to take. Under Governor Edward J. Thye, a Republican, an Interracial Commission had already been established by the legislature, and Thye's successor, Republican Governor Luther W. Youngdahl, ordered the National Guard to desegregate its ranks and pushed for a statewide FEPC; he met resistance in this latter but the support he mustered coincidental to Humphrey's drive for fair employment in Minneapolis indicated that these politicians were not dealing with extreme innovations; imaginative and timely, but not courageous. Minnesota was no Mississippi. Its Negro population was insignificant. Its Jewish population was not.

More was involved here than Humphrey's natural tolerance for the Negro, of which he has an abundance. Humphrey and the city council *talked* Negro, but they also, with embarrassment, meant Jew.

Their tenderness of skin whenever this topic was raised had become much like the hypertenderness shown by southern

businessmen during the early 1960's when outsiders brought
up the subject of bombings in Birmingham and race murders
in Mississippi. They viewed it as a potentially costly, finan-
cially costly, error. The men who ran Minneapolis and who
ran Humphrey were eager to wipe out an ugly aspect of the
city's reputation which had gained national attention. Minneapolis, unlike its sister city, St. Paul, was a cesspool of anti-
Semitism. It was notoriously so.

Writing in *Common Ground* in August, 1946, Carey Mc-
Williams described Minneapolis as "the capitol of anti-Semit-
ism in the United States," a bleakly stratified city in which
Jews were separated from non-Jews by a Midwestern Iron
Curtain. He continued:

> Nor is this iron curtain a matter of recent origin; on the
> contrary, it seems to have always existed. So far as I
> know, Minneapolis is the only city in America in which
> Jews are, as a matter of practice and custom, ineligible
> for membership in the service clubs. In fact, Jews have
> never been accepted into membership in the local Ki-
> wanis, Rotary, Lions, or Toastmasters organizations. . . .
> Even the Automobile Club in Minneapolis refuses to
> accept Jews as members. Mr. Hugh Craig, secretary of
> the club, recently declined to accept the application of a
> well-known and highly respected rabbi. So far as I know,
> there is not another automobile club in America which
> pursues a similar policy. At a recent meeting of the na-
> tional realty boards, the Minneapolis delegation made
> much of the fact that Jews are not eligible for membership
> on the local realty board.

Some stores would not accept job applications from Jews,
some labor unions would not accept their membership. Although there were about 20,000 Jews in Minneapolis, they
played no significant part in the community, being artificially
isolated from its economic and political life. McWilliams
pointed out that in 1938 anti-Semitism had played a significant

part in the defeat of Elmer Benson and the Farmer-Labor Party, for there was underground resentment felt by many Minnesotans toward the Jews who supported him.

The nation, having just finished fighting a war because of Jew-haters elsewhere in the world, began to look askance at Minneapolis, and the city, for the first time in its life, began to feel ill at ease and self-conscious about such matters. The post war growth years were at hand, and Minneapolis wanted its part. So, for economic reasons as well as conscience, it looked inward. A community self-survey was conducted by Fisk University—the first of many such surveys conducted around the country, all patterned after the one in Minneapolis. As a result of this survey, and because of the unfavorable national publicity, and because most importantly the power elite of Minneapolis was smart enough to be flexible (having learned, in the Teamster strikes of the 1930's that rigidity can be disastrous)—the city government moved to clean out at least the more visible signs of bigotry. And in this Humphrey was, so to speak, an eager janitor. He appointed a Mayor's Council on Human Relations, and out of this came the municipal fair employment law in 1947. In the first two years of its operation, the FEPC received complaints from fifty-one Negroes, seventeen Jews, three American Indians, and one Japanese. Half the complaints were thrown out as unfounded, half were settled by a promise to reform, and nobody was taken to court. It wasn't much, perhaps, except as one might compare it with the nothingness of federal action at that time, but nevertheless it was the first such action taken in the nation and Humphrey deserves his share of credit.

Humphrey's next action on behalf of civil rights, however, is questionable both as to value and as to motivation. It did the Democratic Party some good; overnight it made Humphrey a national figure and virtually assured his election to the United States Senate, which he was seeking for the first time that year; but so far as can be measured in retrospect, it did the cause of the Negro no good whatsoever. It could be argued, in fact, that the manner in which he evolved as a headline personality hardened the hearts of the Southerners without at the same time stiffening the purpose of the civil-rights advocates, which is to say that the Humphrey extravaganza at the 1948 Democratic Convention drove the South deeper into its vicious paranoia but was not the beginning of a non southern crusade to correct Negro suppression.

Humphrey was thirty-seven. He had been mayor of the nation's fourteenth largest city not yet four years. And although his job as the state DFL campaign chairman in 1944 had helped, Humphrey's stature at the moment was distinctly limited and rickety. The Republican he was running against, Joe Ball, was unpopular with the unions because of his support of the Taft-Hartley Act and, by backing Roosevelt in 1944, he had lost much favor with the rural Republicans. The strength that remained to him was difficult to estimate but, under the peculiar third-party circumstances in 1948, it might be enough to win unless Humphrey took some dramatic step to cut down the odds. When Ball beat Farmer-Labor candidate Elmer Benson in his senatorial election (356,297 to 213,965) he was greatly assisted by the fact that a Democrat had pulled 78,000 votes that otherwise would have gone to Benson and an Independent Progressive pulled 109,226 votes. In the intervening six years the Farmer-Labor and the Democratic parties had merged, but this still was not enough to assure victory over a Republican (in 1946 the GOP had defeated the DFL candidate) and Humphrey also would be facing the potential of a strong "other" party, such as had helped Ball in '42.

The other party in 1948 would be, of course, the Wallace party. The way to undermine its appeal would be to pull a widely headlined "radical" stunt. Nationally the Democrats were faced with much the same predicament. With Henry Wallace's Progressive Party on the ballot, the liberals of the large urban centers of the north and west might easily go to him in sufficient numbers to leave several normally Democratic states in the hands of Republican Dewey. The presidency of Truman up to that point—with its constant

saber rattling and its establishment of the CIA and its forced
loyalty oaths for government workers and a decided drift
to the right—had done little to inspire the nation's liberals.
They would not vote for Dewey, but they might stay home.
As for the Negroes of the west and north (the only ones who
counted, since southern Negroes couldn't vote), little had
been done by Truman to break what for many was an old
tradition of voting the Lincoln ticket.

Something had to be done to galvanize this drowsy bloc,
and fast. A bit of civil-rights byplay might do it. The thought
did not occur to Humphrey and the northern labor bosses
independently. He had been in the closest touch with some
of them for more than a year. Walter Reuther was by this
time a close ally. (A woman who was one of Humphrey's
secretaries during his mayoralty tells how Humphrey and his
strategy buddies from the University of Minnesota used to
sit around his office by the hour appointing and revising the
cabinet that he would have in that distant day when he would
be President; appointees to the other cabinet posts varied
from day to day, she said, but Reuther was always Secretary
of Labor.) AFL President Green and CIO President Murray
were also very much in on the convention ploy, of course.
As early as the 1947 AFL convention in San Francisco, at
which Green had started a Humphrey-for-Senator boom, the
seed idea of pushing civil rights to hold the north and west
had been planted with Humphrey. And specifically rooting
for him at the Democratic convention were the labor-allied
big city bosses, that odoriferous crew that included Jake
Arvey of Chicago, Frank Hague of New Jersey, and Ed Flynn
of the Bronx.

The plan was for Humphrey to amend the Democratic civil-
rights plank. They did not have to hoke it up in a dramatic
fashion, because that would come naturally. The plank could
not be amended without a fight. The old party regulars, to
whom unity is a sacred word, were against any tampering.

The amendment that Humphrey would seek was drafted by
Joseph Rauh. Rauh is about as radical as Quaker Oats, and the

amendment that he wrote can hardly be differentiated from
the civil-rights plank which the Trumanites had come prepared to offer. The Truman plank called for nondiscriminatory
right to vote, right to work, and equal protection of the laws.
To this, the Humphrey amendment added virtually nothing
except jazzier phrases.

When Humphrey saw that it would split the party, he hesitated. "He was not at all sure what to do," Rauh has said.
"He was reluctant to make a big fight and speech on the
floor." But he was toughened by labor and by the men who
had made him mayor and wanted to make him Senator. He
liked civil rights well enough; only, he was equally motivated
by the desire to be a go-along Democrat, and besides, it was
obvious to him that his amendment added little to the plank.
In this last quibble, however, he had missed the point, as his
counselors soon informed him.

As is common in politics, the substance was not to be the
issue, and was not meant to be; it was the presentation that
counted—the fervency and piousness that would pass for
ideology. For this, Humphrey was just the man. As Arthur
Naftalin, Humphrey's political protégé, later remarked so accurately, "He was not a revolutionary although he *spoke* with
a revolutionary fervor." Then, as now, half of Humphrey was
tone.

The convention platform committee rejected the amendment, Humphrey took the issue to the floor, and won, accompanied by much hurrah. His appeal to the delegates, the
shortest and most remembered speech of his career, contained
one paragraph that virtually invited the Southerners to pull
out: "There are those who say to you—we are rushing this
issue of civil rights. I say we are a hundred and seventy-two
years late. There are those who say—this issue of civil rights
is an infringement on states' rights. The time has arrived for
the Democratic Party to get out of the shadow of states' rights
and walk forthrightly into the bright sunshine of human
rights."

The soon-to-be Dixiecrats trooped out behind their nineteenth-century general, Strom Thurmond. His presidential candidacy on the States' Rights Party ticket was to cost the Democrats thirty-eight electoral votes, all in the South, but this loss was more than offset by the electoral votes from such states as California and Ohio, won by the narrowest margins by Truman, and doubtless won because the liberalism injected into the convention by Humphrey was ballyhooed by the labor leaders when they went home. "Labor did it," said Truman. Wallace's Progressive Party weakened the Democrats in three states, including New York, to the point that the Republicans captured them. But the new, and really we must add fraudulent, role of the Democrats as "fighters for civil rights" kept the Progressives from finding a strong base where they else might have, and this saved Truman.

In Minnesota the same influences destroyed the potential foundation of the demoralized Wallaceites who, splitting with the DFL amid charges that they were pinkos, never were able to seize a radical program to offset the Humphrey-Truman "civil rights" thing, and they wound up with only 28,000 votes—half as many as Eugene Debs had polled in Minnesota twenty-eight years earlier—while Humphrey was defeating Ball 729,494 to 485,801 and Truman was whipping Dewey 692,966 to 483,617. Years later Ball was to say, "Humphrey was no giant killer. I was the incumbent Senator, but I was no giant." And he was correct in putting Humphrey's impressive victory on a different level than merely a candidate-to-candidate confrontation. Quite obviously Humphrey was the more effective campaigner and the more impressive personality, and his personal victory is underscored by the fact that the DFL was not itself influential enough to win the governor's office that year; but the truly significant thing about the size of his victory, the ominous aspect of it, because it pointed to a national trend rather than merely to a Minnesota trend, was that it showed the increasing willingness of the liberal and the middle-of-the-roader to substitute the cause of civil rights for that of civil liberties—and to do so, very likely, without being aware of what was happening. Hum-

phrey's candidacy offered this substitute. Civil rights was to
be the salve for the liberal conscience during the next several
years when civil liberties, banged and buffeted by the Mc-
Carthyites, were not safe to defend. Humphrey and his liberal
and moderate supporters had shown how marvelously effective the substitution could be.

He was not acting in isolation. There was a widespread
retreat, a national retreat by liberals at this time, away from
the beleaguered ramparts. It was a time when even certified
liberals such as Joseph A. Wechsler, now editor of the *New
York Post,* had panicked to the point that they were frantically
churning out pieces for respectable magazines like *Harper's*
on topics such as "How to Rid the Government of Communists," which was the title of his argument in the November,
1947, issue; he seriously advocated barring Communists even
from employment in nonsensitive federal agencies such as the
Labor Department and Fish and Wildlife. Of such stuff was
liberalism made in 1947. Of course, suggestions of that sort
sounded tolerant beside Congressman Rankin's bill to send
a person to jail for ten years for "conveying the impression of
sympathy with Communism or Communist ideology" either
in classroom, private letters, or print. (Humphrey said that,
in principle, he agreed with Rankin.)

Liberals had a problem, of course. How does one retreat
from civil liberties without appearing to be funking out? A
lot of people—liberal politicians, labor unionists, minority
race spokesmen—were illuminated by the same light bulb
almost simultaneously; civil rights, *sí;* civil liberties, *no.* By
going overboard for the cause of civil rights while throwing
the Reds, radicals, and left-liberals to the wolves—not only
as individuals but as officials in *verboten* organizations—they
did very little for civil rights, as the next decade showed only
too painfully, but they greatly weakened the left-of-center
political forces.

Carey McWilliams was as keen an observer as the left wing
had at the time. In his book *Witch Hunt,* published in 1950,

the springtime of McCarthyism, he notes the beginning of this contradictory pitting of civil rights *against* civil liberties as an artificially manufactured phenomenon that

> coincided with the first postwar realizations that a general crisis in the economy was maturing beneath a surface appearance of prosperity and excellent prospects for the immediate future. Determined to avoid if possible a merging of racial unrest and economic disaffection, the strategists of American reaction began to give the appearance of yielding on the subject of racial discrimination while, at the same time, stepping up the pressure against political and economic dissenters. . . .
>
> One could see that the hopeful expectation about a new deal for racial minorities was being encouraged as a cover for a campaign to coerce conformity on economic and political issues. . . .
>
> Confronted with a mounting wave of public indignation on the score of racial discrimination, President Truman was compelled to sponsor a civil rights program for racial minorities; but he was disposed to this course of action, apparently, by his simultaneous discovery that this program could serve as an effective cover for his failure to protect other civil rights—for example, the civil rights of government employees.
>
> The more insistent the nation became that the civil rights of racial minorities should be protected, the more the public appeared to acquiesce in curtailments of the civil rights of economic and political dissenters. The more American Negro leaders, and their liberal allies, affirmed their freedom from economic and political heresies, the more comfortably the opponents of the President's civil rights program settled down to enjoy pleasant filibusters. For the last three years, the general agitation about the civil rights of racial minorities has consistently diverted attention from the extraordinary deterioration

which has taken place in the public's willingness to respect and protect the rights of economic and political minorities.

In Minnesota, the worst Communist witch-hunt in a decade, a witch-hunt led by the very decent liberal Hubert Humphrey and financed by the empire builders of Minneapolis and St. Paul, occurred during the same period in which these partners, the Humphrey liberals and the men of wealth and influence, were beating the gong for fair employment at home and a tougher civil-rights plank in the Democratic platform. Perhaps the most accurate description of their goal would not be civil rights (and certainly not civil liberties) but civil consensus.

This civil rights/civil liberties schizophrenia still exists, one of the best examples being supplied by Arthur Naftalin's actions in July, 1966, as mayor of Minneapolis when seven members of the Minnesota Committee to End the War in Vietnam were arrested in that city under a 1917 anti syndicalist law forbidding more than a certain number of people to gather at any time in public without a U.S. flag. A delegation from the University of Minnesota went to Naftalin to protest. "I'll match my civil-rights record against any of you," he exploded, going into a long story about how he had participated in the 1963 civil-rights march on Washington. Then, returning to the immediate quarrel, he asked, "What were those war protestors doing at 7th and Hennepin?"

Having used the civil-rights theme to gain national notoriety and a seat in the U.S. Senate, Humphrey's zealousness began to cool. Within three months after reaching Washington he was no longer John the Baptist crying in the Democratic wilderness; he had shed his clothing of skins and had outfitted himself in as fine a double-breasted blue suit as Dayton's Department Store had in stock. The new, smooth, unexcited civil-rights advocate revealed himself for the first time on May 3, 1949, in a debate over legislation to supply education money to states. Senator Lodge offered an amendment providing that a state could get the money only if it desegregated its schools. The amendment had been requested by the NAACP. In a wire to Lodge, the NAACP said, "Sound federal legislation in the field of education cannot compromise with the situation. S. 246 without Lodge amendment puts federal government in position of countenancing present inequalities and discriminations because bill in present form gives express approval to 'separate public schools' for minority races." This was an accurate appraisal of the legislation in every respect. It was a subsidy for segregated schools.

The Lodge-NAACP effort was not the kind that is often seen in Congress, killing a bill under the guise of trying to do a greater good. No, Lodge said he intended to vote for the bill, that he favored federal aid to education, but that he was against improving white schools in the poorer states of the South while the Negro schools fell into worse ruin.

When a similar amendment had been offered to a low-income and slum-clearance bill a few days earlier, Senator Paul Douglas, one of the other liberal bulls, opposed it on the grounds that the amendment would drive away the Dixie vote.

Referring to the Douglas argument and bringing it forward to apply to the school-aid bill, Humphrey said that "never on the floor of the Senate has a more pertinent argument, a more logical discussion, and a more courageous stand been taken by one whose heart literally bleeds for those who are the oppressed and who are underprivileged."

Humphrey said he opposed the Lodge amendment on the same grounds—he did not want to lose the Dixie vote. It was strangely high regard for the South's support, coming from a man who only ten months earlier had calculatingly driven the Deep South away from the Democratic convention. Ten months earlier he had cast himself in the role of a heroic purist by disdaining the South's support; he had ridiculed the idea of the preeminence of states' rights. And when Lodge read aloud to Humphrey that passage from his speech ("My friends, to those who say that we are rushing this issue" etc.),

Humphrey brushed aside the remembrance. That was a philosophy, he said, that should be applied only to civil rights in the abstract—to legislation pertaining *solely* to civil rights —not to practical and concrete legislation having to do with housing and education.

Already he was hurrying to patch things up with the South. Oh, yes, he was distraught, he said, that he could not support the civil-rights amendment. "No Senator could be more unhappy than I am at this hour." He likened his pain and agony to that of Christ on the cross, and he called out to God to forgive the segregationists, for "they know not what they do." Still, he was not so distraught that he could not coolly move into a better relationship with the Dixicrats. Ten months earlier—for the benefit of a northern-oriented convention— he debunked the primacy of local initiative. But now, for a southern-oriented Senate, he recalled that as mayor of Minneapolis, he "did not call upon the federal government" to help him in his desegregation program. And he went on to imply, quite clearly, that the federal government should not try to compel local officials everywhere to push for desegregation.

The threat to withhold money from schools might be a very good threat—it might be a very effective threat—but Humphrey said he would prefer not to use it; he would prefer to leave such matters as desegregation up to the initiative of the mayors of, say, Jackson, Mississippi, and Charleston, South Carolina, and other southern officials. He would prefer to leave desegregation to the conscience of Senator Eastland. "I wish every city in America would [desegregate]. But, as much as I detest segregation, I love education more. I believe education is the fundamental answer, in the long run, to the problem of segregation."

Throughout the 1950s and early 1960s, this was also the standard theme of southern segregationist politicians: "education, not integration, is the answer." This pious cant at length prompted Robert Hutchins to suggest that, "Education, not patriotism, has now become the last refuge of scoundrels.")

Although Humphrey admitted that there might be more to civil rights, he still felt that "the most important pieces of civil rights legislation are anti-polltax legislation and anti-lynching legislation, because when men, regardless of race, creed, or color are given full political participation, they will themselves take care of their own problems." It was a far cry from the blanket appeal for total freedom for the Negro that he had demanded at the Democratic National Convention.

As for the concept of a civil-rights amendment being added to ordinary legislation, he had no patience with that. He considered that only a gimmick, a way to embarrass all the sincere liberals under the dome. "A distinguished Negro member of the House of Representatives," Humphrey pointed out in a kind of pouting anger, "said a few days ago that he was sick and tired of having people attempt to attach civil-rights amendments to every bill that came up." (Who? Adam Clayton Powell, in the other House, who in that day was as distinguished a Negro as they had, had just got through warning Washington, "The Negro people will no longer stand for the betrayal of every civil-rights platform." That must have stung.)

Nor would Humphrey listen to the Senators who urged consideration of the amendment as at least a way to put everyone on record. "Whenever any of these questions arise," suggested Senator Ives of New York, "we should not slink away from them, we should not run away from them, we should face them head-on." It was a paraphrase of Humphrey's 1948 convention speech, but he was having none of it in 1949. Instead, he argued, in a cruel hoax that ignored the easily predictable fact that virtually all federal education money going into the South during the next decade would be spent on white schools only, "If the amendment which is now before us were adopted, we would be handing a stone to the Negro who cries out for the bread of knowledge."

In his 1948 convention exhortation, Humphrey had spoken of the nation's "evil patience" toward correcting racial inequalities, but by 1951 Humphrey was saying that although "I refuse to believe that approximately sixty-four or sixty-five Senators who are pledged in their respective states to civil-rights legislation cannot outlast a force half as large, to put it bluntly," still, said he, *"I've learned a sense of patience."* He said he was against putting the economic squeeze on the South to make it change its ways. (In this he was at cross-purposes with the Democratic–Farmer-Labor Party which had sent him to the Senate and which remained, despite his "purge" of its radicalism, a much more progressive body than he represented it to be. In its 1956 convention, the DFL passed a resolution asking that federal funds be withheld from schools not complying with the Supreme Court decision on segregation—something Humphrey would not suggest for another nine years.) The three years he had spent in the U.S. Senate in the companionship of the gentlemen from Dixie had convinced him that the evolutionary way would produce the same results, in due time: "The South is going through a great change in its one-crop agricultural system and in its thinking. As these great economic changes come, you're going to have a change in the political temperament." Have patience.

At the 1952 national convention, at which he was talking softly in the apparent hope to pick up some southern support for his effort to win the vice-presidential nomination, Humphrey said he would "support" but would not "lead" a move to put into the platform a plank opposing a filibuster.

The next year, 1953, Humphrey announced he was willing to compromise with Southerners to get a start on some civil-rights legislation. "I am so distressed over the long stalemate," he said, "that I am perfectly willing to be the compromiser. I am willing to offer the olive branch and get this thing moving. It's better to go a foot than to fail to go a mile." His specific compromise proposal was a bill to set up a presidential civil-rights commission to survey the duties and activities of federal agencies in fields of employment, education, health, housing, and so on. It would have no power of enforcement. It was nothing legislation, or worse than nothing, for it left the false impression that Congress had some concern over civil rights when in fact it had virtually none.

The sagging morale of the liberal bloc—of which Humphrey was by now the recognized leader—was aptly demonstrated at the opening of the 1955 session when it announced that it would stop short of any effort to curb the filibuster that year and would, instead, simply go on record as being upset that filibusters were being used to frustrate civil rights. Senator Lehman had wanted to drive hard, to establish a record and a tradition of militancy, but when Humphrey refused to participate, the move died.

The next year's effort was just as soggy. Former Senator Douglas recalls, "The civil-rights bill was being chloroformed in the Eastland committee in 1956 and I tried to get the House civil-rights bill brought before the Senate, and I only got six votes on that procedural strategy. I was a little hurt—Hubert wasn't one of the six. But, you understand, that was just before the Democratic convention."

Humphrey's forgiveness of the recalcitrant South at the 1956 national convention, where he was again seeking the vice-presidential spot, came through clearly when he worked out, with former Governor John S. Battle of Virginia, a new rule which did not tightly bind the delegates to support the Democratic nominee (if, perchance, he was a civil-rights candidate). Furthermore, since the South was threatening to walk out again if the platform called for White House enforcement of the '54 Supreme Court desegregation order, Humphrey sought only a *court* implementation plank, which came very close to the Jacksonian insult to the court—"They passed it, now let them enforce it."

The hero—to use the word lightly—of 1957 was not Humphrey but Nixon. That was the year that Vice President Nixon gave his opinion at the opening of the session that the Senate could change its rules by a simple majority and that Section 2, of the Senate's famed Rule 22, permitting unlimited debate on rules change, was unconstitutional. Buoyed by Nixon's opinion from the chair, Humphrey and other civil-rights advocates moved to change the rules in such a way that filibusters could be stopped by a simple majority rather than by two-thirds of the members, as at present. Majority Leader Lyndon Johnson, still very much a Jim Crow advocate, moved to table the rules change, and he won. However, Nixon's ruling had given much heart to the civil-rights movement in the Senate (they rallied 36 votes for a filibuster rule change; four years earlier they had mustered only 21). Nixon had not made the ruling without warning. Humphrey had gone to him before the session opened and had said to prepare himself for answering a point of order on ending debates. "Don't get the wrong idea," said Humphrey, "we're not trying to put you on the spot. But if you give the right answer it may make another Abraham Lincoln out of you." Before that conversation ended, Nixon had indicated that he would give the right answer. Later Humphrey tried to pretend that "when I asked for that opinion I was taking a calculated risk," but he wasn't. He knew what Nixon would say.

Humphrey did not again figure in the civil-rights fight in an important way until 1964 when, with a bipartisan consensus that Congress could wait no longer and that it had probably in fact waited much too long, and with Lyndon Johnson now going after the northern Negro and liberal vote to give him an extension of the presidency, Humphrey did give good service in pushing through the civil-rights act of that year.

Then came the 1964 Democratic convention and Humphrey's debated role in supporting/opposing the maverick delegation of Mississippi Freedom Democratic Party protesters who wanted to be seated in place of the all-white delegation from Mississippi. Their argument was that the white delegates were illegally chosen via a Jim Crow election—which was true. Johnson, however, was determined that there would be only peace and harmony, or at least an outward showing of it, on the convention floor, and he was determined to keep the MFDP Negroes in line. He would not himself take part in the manipulations, however. Johnson gave that job to Humphrey. Moreover, he gave him the nasty chore with the heavy implication that if he did not get the Mississippi blacks to settle down and be quiet, he just might not get the vice-presidential spot. All members of the Mississippi Freedom Democratic Party will assure you today that they were sold out by Hubert Humphrey and by Joseph Rauh. Liberals and Negroes will debate this point for a long time.

Rauh was one of the MFDP's attorneys. He held out firm for seating his blacks at first, but then, contending that the MFDP had lost its bargaining position, he urged his Negro clients to accept two "roving delegate" positions. They refused, and strategically it was the only thing they could do —refuse—for they were not there to be compromised but to underscore and dramatize the total subjugation of the Negro in the Mississippi political process. One does not dramatize total subjugation by compromising. And so they refused. And when Rauh kept insisting that they compromise, and finally when he washed his hands of them, they assumed that their honkie attorney had folded up under pressure from his comrade in the ADA, Humphrey. (In their judgment of the quality of the Humphrey-Rauh achievement, the Negroes were no more sarcastic than some reporters who could hardly be called left wingers. Ed Lahey, roving pundit for the Knight Newspapers at that time, wrote of detecting "such an Uncle Tom odor to the Mississippi compromise.")

This is the version of the closed-door dickering given by Mrs. Fannie Lou Hamer, a former sharecropper who lives in Senator Eastland's hometown, Ruleville, and who is, among Negroes, as great a heroine as Eastland is a hero to the segregationists:

MRS. HAMER: "Mr. Humphrey, he kept telling us to compromise for two votes. He seemed *very* upset, very upset. Our attorney at the time told us if we didn't go for the two votes, if we didn't *slow down*, Mr. Humphrey wouldn't get the nomination. [Was it Joe Rauh who told you that?] I *declare* it was Mr. Rauh, and that's what he said. Mr. Humphrey was sitting *right there* when Mr. Rauh said that and he had tears in his eyes—I mean *Humphrey* had tears in his eyes—when Joe Rauh said it. I *'clare* that is the truth. I asked the vice president if his position was more important than the lives of 400,000 black people in Mississippi. He didn't answer me and I didn't get invited to any more meetings, neither. They kept saying we should take two votes *at large*. I couldn't see how that would help us. Dr. [Martin Luther] King said we wouldn't hear of it. They said afterwards that Snick pressured us into refusing the two votes. I tell you, everybody *but* Snick was trying to pressure us. I went to Bob Moses at Snick and he said, 'Mrs. Hamer, you're grown people in Mississippi and you do what you feel is good for you.' So we did. I don't know if Joe Rauh sold us out. But we know *somethin'* happened to us. All I can say besides that is a person can get killed these days for tellin' the truth."

Rauh, on the other hand, denies that Humphrey argued for the compromise to defend his candidacy or was even privy to such arguments. He gets quite angry at the suggestion.

When asked if Humphrey had leaned on him to pull in his horns on the Mississippi Freedom Democratic Party effort, Rauh replied, "This is going to break your heart but that assumption is unfair and absolutely wrong. Humphrey did not lean on me. Hubert Humphrey was the height of ethical standards at that convention. *Johnson* leaned on *him* to lean on me, and he never asked for one concession. As for pulling in our horns, I reject that New Left crap. We didn't pull in our horns. We won. We won more than anybody in the entire place including Bob Moses expected us to get. We got the ouster of the lily whites. We got an offer to recognize, with two delegates from the Mississippi Freedom Democratic Party. We got a promise for the future that is now being implemented. And any suggestion of anybody's pulling in their horns is just New Left rewriting of history. What did you expect them to do, give us unconditional surrender?"

Q. A political friend of yours said that Hubert Humphrey came to you and said, "The conditions of my getting the second place are contingent upon my settling this thing and I need you to help settle it."

RAUH: Everybody told me *except* Hubert Humphrey that he needed to settle it. Hubert Humphrey never said that to me. Half of Humphrey's crowd said that to me. They all were leaning on me the entire time. Kampelman was already blaming me for Hubert's not getting it. Rowe was already blaming me for Hubert's not getting it when they were scared Hubert wasn't going to get it. I never had any doubts in my own mind that he was going to get it.

Q. What did they want you to do?

RAUH: They wanted me to cave in. We never did. We settled on the terms offered me on Sunday. By Tuesday night we had everything we could get. It wasn't everything I would have liked to get but it was everything that convention would give us. It was a goddamned successful meeting. Every night for a week I saw Hubert Humphrey before I went to bed, wanting to get more out of *him*, by pushing him, and he never once said, "Joe, if you'll just stop, I can be vice president." I think Hubert Humphrey at the 1964 convention exhibited the highest political ethical standards I have ever run into in my life.

Q. Simply by not asking you?

RAUH: That's right.

Q. It doesn't take much to get that rating, does it?

RAUH: It doesn't take much to get that rating around this town. Maybe that's right. All I can say is, if I had a chance to be vice president and thereby hope to be president on that route, and I had with me some guy who had been my friend for twenty years, I might very well have succumbed to the temptation to make a remark about "a slight concession on your part and I might be the vice president and then the president." *Never* was that said. I consider that very, very, very high ethical standards. You may say it would be high only by comparison with other things to be seen around this town. Maybe that's right. But I consider it high standards.

On another point Rauh conceded that Humphrey was guilty of undercutting the MFDP position: this was in swinging some of the pro-MFDP people on the credentials committee into an anti-MFDP position. Humphrey and Walter Reuther and ex-Governor Pat Brown of California were among those, said Rauh, who chipped away at their support until he knew the MFDP could not win. To a question on this point, "So Humphrey was in with the others in offering just enough to peel off your support?", Rauh's answer was, in part: "No question about that. That's right. There's other evidence. . . ."

The militant Negroes will not soon forget Humphrey's role in that convention; neither will they soon cease to suspect Rauh of being in cahoots with Humphrey in pressing for a deadly compromise just to help Humphrey's political career, which, as a matter of fact, probably needed no help anyway. At the organization meeting for an important black militant outfit in Washington in early 1968, a reporter asked why there weren't some white liberals in the group, "like, well . . . take Joe Rauh?" To which the blacks hooted and jeered, and advised the reporter, "*You* take Joe Rauh. We found out about him in 1964." More to the point, if there is a point to that convention, they found out something else about Hubert Humphrey.

The Senate Establishment, to which Humphrey had sworn his lighthearted fealty fifteen years earlier, too late had acted to reaffirm the Constitutional rights of the Negroes with special legislation. By the time Congress moved, the Negroes were in something less than a grateful mood, even in respect to liberals such as Humphrey, who had always *said* the right thing and had said it evangelically and sometimes even tearfully. No, by 1964 and 1965 the Negroes had no more trust in politicians named Humphrey than in politicians named Talmadge or Stennis. On March 9, 1965, for example, the protest over conditions in Selma had started quietly, with about a dozen people, mostly black, sitting on the floor outside Attorney General Katzenbach's office in a friendly picnic mood. Chief U.S. Marshal James J. P. McShane had lunches sent up to them. But the mood turned sour and ugly after leaders of the group met with Humphrey. When Reverend Walter Fauntroy, Martin Luther King's Washington representative, urged Humphrey to ask the President to send marshals to Selma to arrest Alabama troopers who were beating Negroes, Humphrey agreed that a few arrests would help, but he argued that "the number of United States marshals is limited and the Justice Department could not easily round up an army of marshals to combat Governor Wallace's state troopers." Other Negro spokesmen said the government wouldn't need more than fifty marshals because they would symbolically represent all the troops at nearby bases. "I can see what you mean," said Humphrey, "but federal troops should be used only as our last ace in the hole." The leaders came out of their meeting with the Vice President to tell the protesters that he had advised them, "Let us wait and see." Humphrey could not have used a worse phrase. Later that afternoon, in a meeting at St. John's Episcopal Church on Lafayette Square, the irritating advice was repeated. "Let us wait and see." By now the blacks could not hear it without becoming enraged, and so they stormed out of the church, ran across the square, and began picketing the White House. Seven hundred were there, and another 120 dashed off to the Justice Department where they acted so rebelliously, chanting and singing and taunting police, that they were dragged out of the building and carried to jail.

Two months later Humphrey was handling another racial boil with similar clumsiness. This time the National Committee Against Discrimination in Housing went to him urging that he put his influence to work on Johnson to convince him of the necessity of extending the 1962 Executive Order to cover *all* federally assisted housing. The Kennedy order of 1962 applied to only about 18 percent. It is within the power of the presidency to do away with discrimination in all housing that is in any way financed by loans from the government or loans secured by the government, which means even ordinary loans from banks covered by federal insurance. The President can simply order it to end, and the various federal agencies must do it (if the Executive rides herd on them). Nothing could be more reasonable. But Humphrey would promise nothing. He said he was "sympathetic." But he refused to say what position he would take with the President. The final decision was up to Johnson; Humphrey could only advocate—but he would not promise to do even that.

When Humphrey became vice president, his old liberal pals in the Senate wondered what he would do about Rule 22. He was the fellow who, throughout his Senate career, had always insisted that each Senate session was a new one at which the Senate could make new rules. Furthermore, it had always been Humphrey's stated opinion that the Senate should be able to cut off a filibuster by a simple majority—and thus the need for the Rule 22 change at the opening of the session.

Now that he was vice president, of course he would rule as he had always said a vice president should rule. Wouldn't he? One morning shortly before he had to decide on it, Senator Douglas said to him, "Well, Hubert, I hope you're studying up on Rule 22."

"Don't worry about that," said Humphrey, grinning. "I've been doing my homework on that one for years."

And so he mounted to the chair to which he had aspired for so many years, a chair of which in previous sessions he had demanded rulings from the brain and from the heart in the hopes of creating a more flexible, responsive legislating body —and he ruled to maintain the status quo, defending the filibuster and all the old rusted lares of the Senate Estab-ment.

The pressures of 1965, the last year in which significant progress was made in civil-rights legislation and also the last year in which the Administration demanded progress, were such that Humphrey began, in his usual way, to split at the seams and go in all directions. On January 29, speaking of people who fight for integration, he said, "You have to be willing to take a stand, and you'll get some victories." Nevertheless, on the same day he also said that the Administration would be willing to "walk the extra miles" with the South in seeking voluntary compliance with the Civil Rights Act provision that bans racial discrimination in federal aid programs. Having shown himself capable of reversing himself 180 degrees within twenty-four hours, he of course found it very simple to change directions from month to month. Thus on May 21 he was again hewing to the hard line, warning the South that the federal government would sue schools to integrate even if they were willing to pass up federal aid. "In reality," he said, "the choice is simply this: to continue receiving federal aid and desegregate or to sacrifice federal aid and desegregate anyway." But by August 26 he was not only turning soft, he was sounding as though he were leaving the fight altogether: "The greatest development in recent American history is the civil-rights movement, but we have about as much civil rights on our statutes as we can get now."

He made it quite clear that when he said this he meant that, for the moment at least, he was going to actively oppose further legislation. His method of demonstrating this new viewpoint (to the dismay of his old liberal friends in the Senate) was in opposing a proposal sponsored by Senator Edward Kennedy to abolish poll taxes in state and local elections, to complement the 24th Amendment prohibition against poll taxes in federal elections. Johnson opposed it, and so therefore did Humphrey.

In December, 1963, James Farmer, then national director of the Congress of Racial Equality (CORE), met with President Johnson to urge the establishment of a national literacy program, aimed primarily at unemployable Negroes. Johnson told him to draft a memorandum on the project, and Farmer did. Johnson telephoned him to congratulate him on the soundness of his idea and to ask for more specifics. The finished project plans were submitted on August 17, 1965.

Four days later Humphrey joined the act by writing Farmer: "The National Cooperative Literacy Program. . . . is an imaginative and constructive concept. You have correctly identified illiteracy as a principal deterrent to economic opportunity . . . . I have asked Mr. Bookbinder [Hyman Bookbinder, Humphrey's liaison man at OEO] to do everything possible to expedite action on the proposal." The following January 10, perhaps believing the program had been funded, Humphrey again wrote Farmer: "Congratulations on your leadership and determination to bring this proposal through to reality. I'm confident that your new assignment will produce a truly historic contribution to our nation." That, however, was unlikely. The program had *not* been funded, was *never* funded, and subsequently, as a result of out-of-sight political strife, died stillborn. The January 10 letter from Humphrey was the last Farmer ever heard from the Executive branch.

A little more than a year later Humphrey was telling Negro leaders that the Irish, the Jews, the Italians and the Cubans who migrated to this country "made something out of themselves without government grants. Why can't Negroes do the same?"

The preeminent test of Humphrey's earnestness about civil rights, however, was taken and soundly flunked by him when, in 1965, he became briefly the Administration's coordinator of all civil-rights enforcement. He was the man with the big stick. All the federal statutes were his to bind together in a fasces and use to force compliance from all government contractors, all businessmen operating in interstate commerce, all schools and universities and highway departments that receive federal funds—the works. He could enforce the National Labor Relations Act provision that prohibits discrimination by trade unions; he could use the Labor Department regulation issued in June, 1963, to decertify any apprenticeship program in which was found discrimination; he could use Title VII of the Civil Right Act of 1964 that bans discrimination in employment; and best of all, perhaps, he had Executive Order 11246 which allows the government to cut off *all* contracts to any company discriminating in its employment—that is, a company operating in Mississippi on a whites-only basis could lose federal contracts not only in its Mississippi plant but also in its Detroit or Seattle plants as well. It is a potentially all-powerful weapon for prying open the employment doors for Negroes.

So what did Humphrey do with this great power?

Nothing. No apprenticeship program was decertified. Not one contract in all the industries that do business with the government and control an estimated 20,000,000 to 25,000,-000 jobs was cancelled.

To say that he has done nothing is not, on second appraisal, quite accurate. He has done what he usually does: he has made speeches. In 1965, at the time he was receiving the powers he would not use, Humphrey said, "It is no exaggeration to say that non-whites, principally Negroes, are on the verge of a major economic crisis. . . . In some neighborhoods the unemployment rate among Negroes is as high as 40 percent." He made very touching speeches.

But by 1968 even these were changing, and on January 21, back in his home town of Minneapolis, he swore a great oath to the Junior Chamber of Commerce that he had no sympathy for the civil-rights militants and vowed that he and others in the Administration would break their backs if they got out of line in the coming summer. Once again he had all the right words and once again his voice broke and his eyes glistened with tears as he spoke of "the Negro mother who simply wants her children to be able to walk safely to a decent school or for the Negro father who wants nothing more than an equal chance to work," etc. He said that decent people understood what the Negroes wanted and he couldn't understand why some Negroes were so hateful about what the government was trying to do for them.

He denounced the Kerner Commission (the presidentially-appointed riot study panel) in the spring of '68 for painting too bleak a picture; he said he was especially resentful of the fact that the panel's report made it sound as if white people have been responsible for holding black people down. He said he was offended by the idea of "group guilt." And he suggested that the Negroes might try to pull themselves up by their own bootstraps, as the Irish and Italians have done.

Still, he could not remain gruff for long, and when a delegation went to him to complain of what they called the "appalling" cuts made by the White House in the "already inadequate" federal funds for job programs in the long, hot summer facing the nation, Humphrey peppily responded that he didn't think the budget "was quite that bad." Yet, he sure wanted to do his part, and would pass their complaints on to the President to see if there was more money for the ghetto unemployed who wanted to be trained. "I was already on the ball team," he told the group jovially. "But now I want to make a home run."

There was no applause.

Making It

The most remarkable achievement of the men who created Humphrey was their passing him off for so many years as the masterful manipulator of party machinery. The insistence of his advisers on casting him as this, a great party engineer, show that most of Humphrey's inner circle are political science Ph.D.'s. Only academicians would think it necessary to portray Humphrey for more than he is, a very articulate, peppy, hard-running officeholder. He operates on personality, as do most successful politicians. Lyndon Johnson knows so little about machine politics or about organizing for a major campaign that it would be embarrassing if he had not also done rather well without the expertise. He operates on a keening line of grudges, favors, special interest leverages, and a sprawling, disjointed network of cronies. There is no organization, no machine about it. They just go, in the words of one successful southern politician, "in a wad." Except for a few surviving city bosses, the same is true of most politicians today; the nearest thing they have to a machine is a personality clique, or a following derived from their power as, say, chairman of a key Congressional committee. So if Humphrey is a poor "organization politician"—and he is—he is in excellent company.

His power in Minnesota politics today is tenuous at best. Clawing his way into the U.S. Senate, he disrupted the hell out of the DFL, but he said it would do the party good if one wing burned down. Today the Republicans control the legislature; they have the governorship; they control the state government completely. The DFL party and the liberal movement in Minnesota are a shambles; they have a hard time electing anyone to the state legislature, much less governor. In the state senate they have a handful; in the house less than a third, and most of that third is from the Twin Cities area. The younger liberals in the DFL distrust Humphrey. They were not around when he was reshaping the party in his own image in the late 1940's, and they see him now mainly as the bucket-carrier for an unpopular President. But, young or old, the consensus in the DFL is that Humphrey was a monumental bungler in the 1966 governor's campaign. At first he would take no sides. Then, after terrible intraparty warfare at the DFL convention at which the nomination was won by Lt. Gov. A. M. Keith, Humphrey gave his vague blessing to Keith and said that Gov. Karl F. Rolvaag, an old Humphrey buddy, should not contest the convention's choice by entering the primary. That, however, was the last assistance Humphrey gave to Keith, and when Rolvaag, disregarding Humphrey's advice, entered the primary against Keith—and defeated him—it was a terrible blow to Humphrey's prestige. Many Keith supporters blamed their man's defeat on Humphrey's failure to help him. And then Rolvaag was defeated in the general election by the Republican and *his* followers blamed Humphrey also for failing to give him the support they expected. Humphrey's role in that election could not have been sloppier. Many Minnesota party leaders now hold him in contempt. Some of this contempt has been loosed in the defection of a number of top officials from supporting the Johnson-Humphrey position on Vietnam; they have publicly sided with the views of their dove senator, McCarthy.

Outside Minnesota he has an even poorer score. He backed losing candidates in New York City and in Philadelphia; he backed the segregationist Governor Haydon Burns for re-election in Florida, and lost; his other excursion into the Deep

South was to throw his arms around such an improbable ally as Governor Lester Maddox of Georgia, a gesture which enraged liberals around the country without gaining any noticeable conservative support. Late in 1967 Humphrey went to Texas in an effort to somehow subdue the famous feud between Governor John Connally and Senator Ralph Yarborough. He called a harmony meeting and gave them a good spiel on party unity. The only trouble was—he had forgotten to invite anyone from the Yarborough camp.

Even when Humphrey possesses a singular propaganda package, he unloads it in such a clumsy fashion that it does him little good in a campaign. The prime example was in December 1958, when he had his eight-hour talk with Khrushchev. This was before a conversation with Khrushchev got to be as common a campaign gimmick as a trip to South Vietnam is today. Humphrey got headlines out of it, all right, but they all blew away before he made good use of them as a buildup for his 1960 campaign. Just out of Russia, with the smell of caviar still on his breath, Humphrey stopped over in London on his way home to declare that he was taking along a personal message from Khrushchev to Ike. "And the message is significant," he assured a news conference. He said Khrushchev told him, "I'm now going to tell you a secret." And, after telling it to him, said Humphrey, Khrushchev added, "And now I'm going to tell you another." Yes, yes, said the reporters —now give us a hint of what the secrets were about, just a clue. Oh no, said Humphrey, "You couldn't pry the secrets out of me with a crowbar. . . ."

Two days later, back in Washington, he said the use of the word "secrets" was maybe "a little unfortunate." And in another two days, Ike said that what Humphrey had told him of Khrushchev's views on the Berlin crisis, at that moment the hottest topic around, "was not particularly new." Nevertheless, for a few days Humphrey was making the most of the fact he had spent the day with the Russian premier, no matter if all they discussed was the weather; in his first six days back in America, Humphrey made five public speeches before 15,000 people and appeared on four network radio-TV programs.

But somehow it all came through as rather trivial, like a family's vacation film. And by the time Khrushchev, early in February, 1959, snickered in his roguish way, "It is laughable to suppose that I could have confidential relations" with Humphrey, most Americans had ceased caring. So maybe Khrushchev was right in likening Humphrey to Baron Munchausen. Or maybe Humphrey was right in interpreting Khrushchev's attack on him as indicating "a high degree of insecurity in the relationships between Soviet Russia and the Communist Chinese." Most spectators had a hard time working up much enthusiasm for this return bout between a couple of old middleweights.

Then one must recall his pitiful showing in the 1952 and 1956 national conventions (at the latter he was just *sure* he had the vice-presidential nomination sewed up, and then Adlai threw it open to the convention and on the first ballot Humphrey's eventual fate was determined. He trailed Senators Kefauver, Kennedy and Gore, and Mayor Robert Wagner of New York; Humphrey, the sure thing, was fifth). These episodes show in only too human terms that Humphrey is an emoter, not a machinist. He is a slapdash organizer. When it comes to whooping it up and sounding trumpets for the faithful, he excels, but he has little talent for the tough kremlinizing of a campaign or of a party. He was once asked how he ran a campaign, and his answer was, "Oh, I don't know, just get around and get people interested."

He is not entered in any of the presidential primaries this year, and that is just as well. They have always been his bane. In the 1956 primary Kefauver upset Stevenson in Minnesota and thus prevented Humphrey from going to the Democratic National convention as a delegate. Piqued by that, Humphrey encouraged the DFL to join Minnesota conservatives to repeal the state's presidential primary law. (Progressives originally championed such primaries to reduce the power of vested interests by enabling the people, instead of the party bosses, to choose state delegates to the national conventions.)

But four years later, in 1960, Humphrey was again to run against the primary wall, and this time with even more disastrous results. He was courageous in a way, but he was also dumb, and he was very much a patsy. His 1960 pursuit of the presidency was badly managed, conceived without imagination, and woefully under-financed. He was the first candidate to declare, and the first to drop out. He stayed in just long enough to be thoroughly butchered by John F. Kennedy. (The traumatic effects on Humphrey of his treatment at the hands of the Kennedys have never really worn off. A bitter dislike for that clan is one of the things that bound him so firmly to that other Kennedy-hater, LBJ. It took Humphrey a long time to get over the fact that in 1960 Orville Freeman went for Kennedy at the national convention when he, Humphrey, wanted to hold out the Minnesota delegation. Thus in 1964, when "Rural Americans for Johnson and Humphrey," the main citizens group for non-urban campaigning in that election, wanted to prepare a major radio show featuring Humphrey and Freeman, Humphrey's office sent word, "Hell no, we won't appear with that goddamn Freeman, and furthermore, he won't be secretary of agriculture much longer." But because Johnson did not want to appear to be weeding out Kennedy appointees, Freeman was kept on, and eventually he and Humphrey made up again.)

Humphrey, because of his reputation as an outspoken liberal, and Kennedy, because of his Roman Catholicism, were forced down the treacherous primary route to the presidency to demonstrate their popular appeal to party leaders.

Humphrey thought he would do well in Minnesota's neighbor, Wisconsin, a state where he was well known and which shared a similar progressive political tradition. After a disorganized start, he captured four of ten congressional districts and came close in several others. It was enough to cushion his defeat and frustrate Kennedy, who, although he

won the primary by more than 100,000 votes and claimed
Humphrey was Wisconsin's "third Senator" in order to inflate
his achievement, was nettled by the way his victory was received in the press.

"The newspapers took our victory away from us in Wisconsin," a Kennedy aide said. "We didn't win by the margin they
had predicted, and they pointed to evidence of a Protestant-
Catholic division among voters, which meant the religious
issue was still alive and kicking. So we had to win in West
Virginia. We were praying Humphrey wouldn't drop out."

Humphrey obliged, fulfilling the crucial role described for
him by another Kennedy aide: "If Hubert Humphrey didn't
exist, we'd have had to invent him." Without Humphrey to
keep his bandwagon rolling by subduing the religious issue
in predominantly Protestant West Virginia, it is unlikely that
Kennedy could have captured the Democratic presidential
nomination. Kennedy and his aides had been eying West Virginia for several years. In 1958, they dispatched Louis Harris,
the New York pollster, to feel the political pulse. The results
were encouraging: 52 percent of those polled favored Kennedy over Richard M. Nixon. Another Harris poll in December, 1959, showed Kennedy winning over Humphrey in West
Virginia with 70 percent of the vote (Catholics, 92 to 8 percent; Protestants, 67 to 33 percent for Kennedy). In early
1959 Kennedy and his brothers began mobilizing West Virginians to establish a statewide volunteer organization.

Kennedy recognized that the West Virginia primary would
be meaningless unless he had an opponent to defeat and thus
demonstrate that in a heavily unionized border state Protestants would vote for a Roman Catholic. So he soft-pedaled
his interest in the West Virginia primary until Humphrey
took the bait and challenged him to enter. In the spring of
1960 Kennedy and Humphrey, who had sat beside each other
in the gentlemanly calm of the U.S. Senate, plunged into the
factional maze of West Virginia politics. In Humphrey's Minnesota, personalities and issues tend to dominate a wide-open
style of politics. Kennedy, however, came to West Virginia

with experience in rough-and-tumble politics. He received his basic training in Massachusetts where politics bears some similarity to the West Virginia brand, with disciplined organizations providing election-day insurance.

The Wisconsin campaign left Humphrey $75,000 in debt as he headed for the coal fields where money speaks louder than oratory in politics. In West Virginia, the traditional electioneering techniques of the city machines that thrive in a Boston or Chicago are modified to fit the state's rural environment. "It takes money," a West Virginia politician explained. "You buy the organization just like you would if you were going to build a house and hired carpenters, electricians, and plumbers. And most of the money is spent legally —on hiring cars (to haul the scattered rural populace to the polls) and precinct workers." Some of it also is spent illegally, buying the votes of poor whites and Negroes in a dozen counties with cash or half-pints of booze.

Humphrey, who didn't believe West Virginia's county organizations could turn out the majorities they claimed until the results were in, gambled that his liberal voting record on domestic issues and Kennedy's religious handicap would combine to give him a cheap victory. Humphrey also counted on the international labor unions, which he had served faithfully in Congress, to contribute enough funds so he could conduct a respectable campaign. But the unions and their friends, determined to end up on the side of the Democratic presidential nominee, refused to give Humphrey any funds and some even pressured him to withdraw. The fearful neutrality of most of the international unions effectively restrained their West Virginia locals, which also lack the machinery to turn out the vote on a scale to compete with the Democratic county organizations.

As a result, Kennedy spent at least $250,000 to Humphrey's $30,000 in the West Virginia primary (Humphrey described the Kennedy money as compounding into a "short-term area redevelopment program for West Virginia"). "The Massachusetts Senator bought a landslide not an election," observed

W. E. Chilton III, publisher of *The Charleston Gazette*. "At the outset Kennedy contracted with factional organizations in machine-controlled counties where money talks. . . ." Most Democratic and Republican leaders in the state agreed that Kennedy, who frankly admitted his campaign cost a lot of money because he had to overcome voter uneasiness about his religion, had not bought the election.

Money is fundamental in politics, but what makes the difference is how a candidate spends it. Humphrey, operating on what he called "a shoestring cut in half," failed to effectively utilize the little funds he had. His first plunge into national politics raised questions about his managerial ability to organize and direct a campaign on unfamiliar political terrain. One of the West Virginia campaign cochairmen that Humphrey selected told a newsman for a national magazine that he preferred Stevenson and Senator Stuart Symington to Humphrey as the Democratic presidential nominee. Kennedy used this incident as proof that Humphrey was nothing but a stalking horse for other candidates. Humphrey's advance work, essential to turning out good crowds for political rallies, was wretched. In Charles Town, Humphrey spoke to 200 persons. The next night Kennedy addressed 2,500. A television debate with Kennedy gave Humphrey one of his few opportunities to reach a statewide audience. But Humphrey muffed it by leading off with a statement suited more for a national audience while Kennedy made a persuasive, provincial appeal.

His ineptness in handling campaign fundamentals contrasted with Kennedy's brilliance in stealing the very images that Humphrey had counted on to carry him to victory in West Virginia. The national press greatly exaggerated religious bigotry in the state, which enabled Kennedy, despite his lavish campaign expenditures, to win the underdog role from Humphrey. Franklin D. Roosevelt, Jr., campaigning for Kennedy, became living proof to loyal New Deal West Virginians that Kennedy, who in contrast with Humphrey had shunned the liberal label, represented FDR's second coming.

Humphrey watched helplessly as his own political images were usurped by Kennedy—even to the extent that West Virginia Negroes overwhelmingly voted for JFK because they identified with his religious handicap despite Humphrey's stronger civil-rights record.

Humphrey, unlike Kennedy, also acted as if he weren't convinced that he could become president. His campaign buttons read "It's Humphrey in '60," an unimaginative slogan which was chosen so the buttons could be used in his Minnesota senatorial campaign if his bid for the presidency failed. "Most people realized what Humphrey knew himself—he couldn't become President," a West Virginia labor leader observed. Kennedy capitalized on this sentiment by stressing that Humphrey wasn't a serious candidate but only a front man for others. Therefore, Kennedy argued, West Virginians had been given a rare historical honor of voting for him and thus choosing the next president (polls showed him defeating Richard Nixon), who thus would do everything in his considerable power to aid their state.

"Why, there's nothing going on here, nothing at all," Lyndon Johnson smugly remarked to a reporter during his only appearance in West Virginia while Humphrey and Kennedy were hustling for votes. There is no question that LBJ was cheering Humphrey on, hoping that he would stop Kennedy in West Virginia and thus give Johnson a better shot at the presidential nomination. Symington jokingly remarked that Johnson and he would be running for president as long as there was a breath of air in the body of Hubert Humphrey.

Humphrey was constantly on the defensive, denying Kennedy's charge that he was just a tool in a cynical effort by Johnson, Symington, and others to gang up and deny JFK the presidential nomination. Johnson ignored warnings that a Kennedy victory in West Virginia would bury his candidacy, although at the last minute LBJ rushed in oil money from Texas in a futile attempt to buy Humphrey some organizational support (it came too late to do much good). Johnson thought the real prize in West Virginia was the twenty-five state delegates to the Democratic National Convention and he predicted twelve of them would support him. But Kennedy captured fifteen of the delegates. They weren't bound by the primary results, but they were a persuasive coup. This was the extremely important effect of Kennedy's victory, that it converted hesitant party leaders in such key states as Michigan, New York, and Pennsylvania who gave him the votes he needed to win the nomination on the first ballot.

"Vote me up or vote me down, but vote me up or down on the issues," Kennedy urged West Virginia Democrats. The only trouble with that advice was the impossibility of finding an issue of substance between Humphrey and Kennedy. If there was a bona fide issue in the West Virginia primary, neither Humphrey nor Kennedy found it after a month of strenuous campaigning. Their only disagreement was over who should be president. Both promised, once in the White House, to pursue the standard liberal solutions to the problems of depressed areas.

In the affluent 1950's, West Virginia's economy discarded surplus coal miners and marginal farmers by the thousands. In 1950, only 4.8 percent of the state's labor force was unemployed—the same as the national average. Eight years later West Virginia's unemployment rate was the highest in the nation. Joblessness had climbed to 14 percent, almost double the national average of 7.2 percent in the 1958 recession. In the southern coal-mining counties, unemployment was swallowing almost 30 percent of the labor force. From 1950 to 1959, the state lost 106,000 jobs.

The great American promise—work for anyone who wanted it—proved to be an Indian giver in West Virginia. The mining of coal had become an occupation principally for machines rather than men. In the peak employment year of 1948, almost 125,000 men helped extract West Virginia's underground riches. But in the next eight years while coal production declined 11 percent, coal-mining employment dropped 42 percent. Today only about 40,000 miners are needed to make West Virginia the nation's largest coal producer.

In their wake, the machines left a bewildered mass of job-less humanity whose families for decades had known only coal and how to mine it. The fifties would be remembered by them not as a decade of peace and prosperity, but as the time when their lives no longer had purpose or value. Almost 450,000 of them left West Virginia in search of work. The state's population declined 7.2 percent to 1,860,421 from 1950 to 1960—the greatest population loss of any state.

Thousands also remained in the desolate, half-boarded up coal camps which blemish West Virginia's natural beauty. They were without work and increasingly without hope. (Unemployed miners described the boards in coal camp windows as Eisenhower curtains.) Hitchhiking excursions across the country turned up few jobs. And hundreds of their relatives who had found work in Akron or Cleveland were knocked back into their native hills when the rhythm of the business cycle tapped out the 1958 recession. When a new chemical plant near Point Pleasant announced it would ac-cept applications for two hundred jobs, about 4,000 men showed up to stand in line on a cold winter day—creating the worst traffic jam in the Ohio River town's history.

At one time or another, 300,000 of the state's citizens de-pended wholly or partly on surplus government food com-modities to stay alive. One of every six school-age children lived with or in a family that was on welfare. Until 1961, West Virginia provided no public assistance payments to able-bodied men who couldn't find work but had exhausted their unemployment compensation benefits. Only surplus com-modities, considered nutritionally inadequate in the fifties, kept them and their children alive.

Thus Humphrey and Kennedy in West Virginia confronted a microcosm of impending national problems: the continuing rural exodus to the slums of overcrowded metropolitan centers and the sharp impact that automation is having on private employment. Their solutions to these problems advanced dur-ing the primary were timid and involved only harmless tinkering with a status quo that had indifferently discarded thousands of West Virginians as if they were nothing more than obsolete pieces of machinery.

Both Humphrey and Kennedy championed accelerating national economic growth and a new program of federal aid to begin rebuilding depressed areas, which President Eisenhower vetoed. They also favored more research to find new uses for coal, immediate relief for the unemployed, and an expansion of other federal programs to aid West Virginia. Humphrey proposed establishing a Youth Conservation Corps (which later became part of the Job Corps). And he became excited about mine-mouth power as the solution to the state's problems—building power plants near mines to burn coal to generate electricity that would be sent by wire to distant metropolitan centers. Private utilities already were doing this in West Virginia. But it is evident that mine-mouth power plants alone will never save the state. Their enormous capital investment pays off in relatively few jobs because of automation. And they require large quantities of cooling water, which means they would usurp the most developable valley land while creating air and water pollution problems.

West Virginia revealed Humphrey's limitations as a national campaigner, but much more importantly it showed the impotence of his liberalism in developing even an ad hoc vision of how to move beyond the New Deal's wax museum and toward a good society in an age of automation and creeping affluence.

Mankind: A Cause Heard Round The World

Humphrey gained quite a reputation for his advocacy of disarmament, a reputation he deserved because he worked on the problem at a time when only two or three men in Congress were interested in it at all; he had no competition for the leadership of the disarmament study group in the Senate. By keeping the topic somewhat fresh in that chamber, by periodically firing off a few of his ringing commonplaces— "Joe Louis didn't have to hit everybody in the snoot when he walked down the street to prove to them he was heavyweight champion," or "The amount of destruction that is contemplated in the first hour [of an atomic attack] is enough to give everybody psychiatric pneumonia for the next twenty years, out of the chill it would give them," or "It is a beautiful day outside; I see no reason we should have so many clouds in our inner thoughts here"—Humphrey did keep the mind of the Senate from solidifying in some kind of belligerently grotesque posture, and did keep his colleagues thinking in terms of power alternatives and of negotiations. Thus he can justifiably take some credit for having held off senatorial psychic sclerosis long enough to enable his colleagues to receive favorably, in 1961, President Kennedy's proposal for the establishment of an Arms Control and Disarmament Agency (twenty-four days before he also announced a military buildup and increased defense spending, which was typical of the late President's split personality). This transaction is a good example of how little it takes to be a hero, how little it takes to be considered "influential" in the liberal ranks. Senator Joe Clark tells it this way: "It seemed to me that Hubert was largely responsible for getting the Arms Control and Disarmament Agency. I remember very well when the vote came on the floor I wanted to stiffen it and I got to my feet to do so. It was originally called the disarmament agency. George Aiken moved to make it the arms control and disarmament agency. I was against that because I was one of these guys that thought you had to go the whole way. Anyway, disarmament encompassed arms control, and I felt we would denigrate the agency if you put arms control in the title. So he, Hubert, hurried over to me and said, 'For God's sake, don't do that [oppose Aiken's proposal]. We've had trouble enough getting this thing out of Foreign Relations. The chamber is loaded with people who don't want this at all. We'd better have Aiken on our side.' So I said, 'All right, goddamnit,' and sat down. By voice vote they changed the name and then the thing slipped through all right. I may give him too much credit but to me he was a hero in this thing."

Then two years later, in 1963, when Senator Thomas J. Dodd prepared a resolution urging President Kennedy to offer the Soviet Union a limited test-ban treaty, Humphrey first and then thirty-two other senators coauthored it, and this prepared the atmosphere in which the treaty was successfully fashioned later that year, the Senate vote being 80 to 19. Because the Senate must ratify such treaties, Humphrey's disarmament talk over the years was, like pillow learning, influential. But his role can be judged accurately only when it is put up against the years of constant study and discussion and negotiation and letter-writing on the part of numerous United Nations groups, who got little enough encouragement, on balance, from either the U.S. State

Department, the Congress, or Presidents Eisenhower and Kennedy.

The Eisenhower of the 1950's who "oozes good will," as Humphrey once said a bit disparagingly and quite inaccurately, used well his talent for doing nothing at several points when another president might have been tempted to act foolishly tough; and to this inherited proof that not all U.S. presidents need lose their heads during crises, the new, young President added the sweep and verve of his speeches on disarmament to the United Nations and at American University—the shining effects of which were somewhat smudged by our needless resumption of atmospheric nuclear testing in his first year, but which nevertheless carried with them the Kennedy sporting appeal. The Eisenhower equanimity plus the Kennedy flair had much more to do with tipping Washington toward an acceptance of the test-ban treaty than anything Humphrey ever did; and, in fact, a greater influence than anyone or anything in this country was the fact that by mid-1960 the Soviet propaganda barrages on behalf of their disarmament proposals were causing concern in Washington and were stirring editorial criticism across the country aimed at both the Eisenhower Administration and Congress for their almost total indifference to the need for intensified research into the disarmament problem. Russia was stealing the show around the world. In 1957 and 1958 Humphrey's subcommittee had urged the State Department to "keep the disarmament ideas flowing through the pipeline," but of course the State Department had acted with its usual lethargy and Humphrey's group chided them in the mildest fashion, hardly in a way to get action from that drugged bureaucracy. Typical of Humphrey's disspirited style was this underestimate made before the Senate Appropriations Committee, in June, 1960, in which he hardly seems aware of the enormity of the thing he is protesting: "There are signs that, either through inaction or inability, we are permitting the weapons development race to proceed much faster than the race for effective means of control." Whatever effect this sort of Mr. Chips statement had on the U.S. Senate, it had no effect on the State Department.

Over the years, Humphrey had raised a thousand questions, but he had answered few, and he was constantly tripping over political quibbles. In 1956, an interim report on recent hearings before the Senate Disarmament Subcommittee, which he headed, questioned whether nations engaged in an arms race costing $100 billion a year could order sudden, drastic disarmament without harming their economies; it grimly stated that the rapid development of powerful new weapons made armament control "vastly more complicated and perhaps impossible"; it questioned whether President Eisenhower's appointment of a special assistant on disarmament was the "most effective" method for handling "relevant information on disarmament policy, for formulating that policy and for executing it" (this was probably meant only as a political dig for home consumption, since Ike's special assistant for disarmament was Harold E. Stassen, former governor of Minnesota and a Humphrey foe); it sniffed at a United Nations group, which was at that time attempting to solve many of the same problems, and wondered critically if it really was possible to consider disarmament without considering the political questions arising from it—which, said the Humphrey report, the UN did not do.

Mostly good questions and reasonable doubts—but little constructive advice. But the report was not in vain; he had squeezed it out swiftly enough to be in time for his try for the 1956 vice-presidential nomination. Of course, he couldn't have been serious about the report's serving as a working paper for the Senate, since he had released it without first letting the Republicans on the subcommittee see it—including such important, although backward, members as Styles Bridges and William Knowland, who immediately squawked, and the proposal for disarmament was thereby reduced to a partisan issue.

As Disarmament Subcommittee chairman, Humphrey would, infrequently, call a meeting and summon spokesmen for the State and Defense departments, and sometimes also call in a university psychiatrist, and they would chew over some of the general things that had been reported on the disarmament problem by newspapers and magazines; they were not so concerned by the belligerent tilt of the world's axis that they could not, now and then, even pause for a contemplative discussion of an essay by Reinhold Niebuhr on whether atomic weapons would be more of a deterrent to global conflict than was Nobel's dynamite. Seldom did these hearings have more focus than a gentlemanly bull session. For anything more than a surface grasp of the problem, Humphrey relied on his staff; he himself, having scattered his time and interests over a dozen legislative topics, never took the time to become the kind of authority on disarmament that Richard Russell was on armament. ("I think he was more enthusiastic than learned," is the kind way Senator Clark puts it.)

As late as 1960—after a decade in which most Sunday newspaper supplements had carried stories about how the Communists' atomic testing could be detected by seismic devices, and after Humphrey himself, asleep or awake, had sat through several hours of testimony by government witnesses on seismic detection—he was still asking, "Isn't the signal similar to the earthquake signal, as some people say?"

Humphrey's torrent of good ideas sometimes canceled one another out. He agreed with President Eisenhower that Red China should be brought into any disarmament discussions; but, unable to brake the momentum of his thoughts, he then flashed into excess, taking the position that "Frankly, I don't think this nation could afford to talk sincerely about real disarmament until we get China in on it. I think it would be very dangerous to agree to have a disarmament agreement including the Soviet Union, the United States, the United Kingdom, France, and Western Germany if you are going to ignore 650 million people who have learned how to shoot and kill and to run modern machines of war." Inasmuch as there was not then (this was 1959) even the slenderest thread of diplomatic contact between the United States and Red China, he was in effect ruling out a disarmament agreement of any kind between this nation and any other major antagonist, which was certainly a questionable position to take in light of the fact that Red China had (and still has) virtually no air force, had no nuclear weapons, and still has no adequate missile system for carrying nuclear warheads. Furthermore, the Chinese seemed mainly propelled toward developing these things out of a quite proper feeling of being at the mercy of Russia and the United States, a feeling that would have been somewhat dissipated by an honest move toward disarmament by these major powers.

Nor did Humphrey's logic always hit the mark. In the 1960 hearings of the Subcommittee on Disarmament, he complained to a Pentagon witness: "You know it is a peculiar thing around here, you can get an extra billion dollars for a B-70 program, but it is difficult to get $10 for a disarmament program." He added, "I happen to think we need both." He did not really mean that he favored both at a ratio of one to ten million, of course; but his meaning was just about that unnerving, being a variation of the threadbare thesis of every happy reprobate, that the most dramatic salvations are reserved for the greatest sinners. "Many people don't quite understand this," he said, "but I don't think you disarm unless you are armed." It sounded like the very sort of disarmament the Pentagon could go for, and John N. Irwin II, then Assistant Secretary of Defense for international security affairs, leaped on it: "The Defense approach to disarmament, as a whole, is quite the one you just mentioned, Mr. Chairman. We believe you have to be well armed before you can disarm." With that open-end reformation in mind, the Pentagon has, since those hearings eight years ago, increased its armament budget by about 100 percent. Humphrey has not been heard to protest.

Spooked by the Communists of Europe, Humphrey was consistently a supporter of heavy military budgets—much heavier than Eisenhower wanted or asked for. In 1954, when

Ike announced a plan to cut the armed forces by 430,000 over the next eighteen months and to halve the draft calls, Humphrey was appalled. "Are we more concerned about a deficit or the power and potentiality of the enemy," he asked. That was the year he cosponsored an amendment introduced by Senator John F. Kennedy to give the Army an additional $350 million over what President Eisenhower requested (it was defeated 50–38 by forty Republicans and ten Democrats and somehow the nation survived). Even worse, Humphrey has promoted the fantasy that civil defense is possible against thermonuclear war. In 1959, he announced that a comprehensive civil disaster manual had been printed at his request by the Senate Government Operations Committee. Three years later he voted against an amendment to kill a $93.8 million appropriation for civil defense, which largely provides useless jobs for political hacks from city hall to the Pentagon.

For a supposed devotee of disarmament, Humphrey certainly kept the air full of threats.

He was in the group that sounded the perpetual fear of the missile gap, or the submarine gap, or the armed forces gap.

In 1957, when the Russians were already fearful of what we had in mind by our NATO nuclear policies and by rearmament of Germany, he sloshed some gasoline on the fire by saying that the United States will never conclude a disarmament agreement with the Soviet Union until it can "bargain from strength—the only bargaining Russia respects." He damned Eisenhower for weakening the military establishment, warned that "people are being lulled into believing everything is jolly—it isn't," and thundered with all the sad belligerency of a shorn Samson, "No Soviet navy ever entered the Mediterranean while Harry Truman was President!"

In 1958 he berated Ike for the unilateral cutting of America's defense forces. Perhaps to compensate for the fact that from his Senate race in 1948 to his presidential primary race in West Virginia in 1960, he had to put up with charges of sitting out World War II, Humphrey has always been a hawk.

Not once in his Senate career did he through amendment or through organized debate attempt to correct the lopsided ratio of defense versus domestic spending in the budget.

As soon as it had been noted in Washington that Humphrey had but one inflexible and automatic response to Communism, he was put to use by the policymakers. Surrendering his place on two committees vital to his constituents (Labor and Agriculture) in order to make the switch, Humphrey went on the Foreign Relations Committee as a confirmed Truman-Acheson-Harriman hard-line Cold Warrior; he took the new seat at their request, and with the agreement of then Minority Leader Johnson, having met with them all in the White House a few days before Truman left office in January, 1953. It was understood that his vote could be counted on, and he stuck to his bargain of helping to perpetuate their policy of anti-Communist absolutism to the extent that this was possible under a somewhat hostile administration. His mentors pointed Humphrey eastward, for the hard line at that time was concentrated in Europe, not in Asia.

Even as late as 1965, when almost everyone but the generals had dismissed NATO as a Cold War antique, Humphrey was cheering it on. "We must maintain and strengthen NATO in the face of Soviet military presence which changes but does not wither," he declared, although intercontinental ballistic missiles make a Soviet invasion of Western Europe appear to be a quixotically antiquated threat.

In his first years in the Senate, when he was more interested in agricultural prosperity than in defense prosperity, he had indeed looked to Asia as a proper place to fight the hunger that drove nations into Communism. "Our Atlantic Pact and European recovery programs," he said in 1949, three months after getting to Washington, "are only half the fight. Let us turn around and face our other friends and bring them into the councils of the free and help them to a standard of living that can truly make them free. The people rising to greatness and strength are there, in Asia and Africa. . . . The future lies across the Pacific. We are letting the future escape

us until we recognize the fact." He was talking especially
about aiding India.

Humphrey, who truly believes in what Wilson called "the
righteous conquest of foreign markets," is an articulate
advocate of overseas economic expansion as essential to
American prosperity (U.S. exports in 1965 provided jobs
for 2.9 million Americans—4.7 percent of total private employment). "We must expand our exports," Humphrey argues
in *The Cause Is Mankind.* "We have simply failed to win our
share of world markets for American products. . . . We have
built great factories and plants—and now hundreds of them
stand idle. Increasing our exports will help solve the problem. . . ." (Of course, Humphrey did not write this book; he
passed that chore along to an aide. But he must have read it
and approved of it before it went out under his name, so it
is a proper source for such quotes.)

He also champions foreign aid as both a subsidy to American business (its recipients generally are required to use U.S.
funds to buy U.S. products) and as a foot-in-the-door so that
American businessmen can capture more foreign markets.
Foreign trade and aid, as Humphrey and the American establishment envision it, inevitably involve the United States in
foreign conflicts to protect its trading territories.

Having joined the Foreign Relations Committee, he added
a tough military side to his personality, aimed at Europe.
To fight off the Communists in Europe, a stiff lip and sacri-
fices were quite in order. Late in 1951, just returned from
Europe, Humphrey said the United States defense and foreign
aid programs "obviously mean that the social programs many
of us like will have to be held in abeyance or get under way
in a moderate manner. Let's be frank about it, and say some
things must wait." But fighting the Communists in Asia at
that time interested him only in partisan flurries, as in supporting Truman over the defense of Formosa. In 1950 he said
(quite accurately) that "Americans don't know much about
Southeast Asia and are making a lot of mistakes. We identify
with their [the French] bad past of colonialism and ex-

ploitation [in Indochina, now called Vietnam]." Noting that
this country was supporting Bao Dai in Indochina against
Communist-trained forces led by Ho Chi Minh, he said, "Bao
Dai has been on the banks of the Riviera during the past
months, while Ho has been leading the fight. We are backing
Bao Dai. I suggest we look for another choice—identify our-
selves with native, liberal, positive leaders from their own
people." The idea of participating in a big war in Asia made
him shiver. "To plunge headlong into the Soviet trap of fighting a major war in Asia," he told the St. Paul *Pioneer Press* on
April 15, 1951, "is outright political stupidity and national
suicide." Nevertheless, wherever there was war, including that
messy one in Korea, he gave his total trust to the military, as
he was to do later in regard to the Vietnam conflict. The idea
of fighting in Asia was so offensive to him, and his simple
willingness to leave the Korean rumpus to the machinations
of the Pentagon mind, made him almost sound willing to forget
the whole thing. In May, 1951, he complained to the ADA,
"Congress is momentarily immobilized. It has temporarily
taken over the responsibilities and prerogatives of West Point
without having completed the difficult course of study. Congress should stop trying to play Napoleon and Caesar and
Alexander the Great and get down to legislating. It is derelict
in its public responsibilities and duties while it debates how
to get a quick and easy victory in a most difficult place under
most difficult circumstances." Three years later his interest in
Asia had not noticeably increased. In April, 1954, he joined
with Hickenlooper in warning Eisenhower that he had better
not have any ideas about sending troops to Indochina without
first processing the decision through "appropriate committees
of Congress." And the next month, while super-anti-Commu-
nist Paul Douglas was arguing that the Red conquest of Indochina would be a "catastrophe" that would pull down other free
nations, Humphrey was contending that there was no need to
send United States troops to that country because French and
native forces were sufficient (that was the year, by the way,

that the French capitulated). But 1954 saw no lessening of his harshness toward European Reds. In December of that year, when Secretary of Agriculture Ezra Taft Benson proposed selling butter and other surplus farm products to Russia and other countries behind the Iron Curtain, the archreactionary Willis Robertson of Virginia observed coldly, "I can't see how it would be to our advantage in the long run to give the Russians a better standard of living," and Humphrey agreed: "We ought to see how we can improve the trade picture with friends before trying to improve it with our enemies." And he was still holding firm to this position in 1956 when Ike asked Congress to lift the ban on selling surplus wheat, cotton, and similar commodities behind the Iron Curtain. The Senate Agriculture Committee turned him down, Humphrey (who by now had regained a seat in that body) being among the dissenters, saying that Ike had "made only a recommendation but no justification" for the policy. "On the basis of what I know to date," said Humphrey, "such sales would be harmful to our interests in the anti-Red struggle." Later he would change and favor doing business with Russia. That was after the Democratic policymakers had picked him up and turned him around to face the Pacific and after big agriculture and big business had told him firmly that they needed the Iron Curtain markets.

When he felt that his position as President Johnson's alter ego required him to see Asia as virtually living under the threat of a giant red squid, he rushed to obey, but he was not equal to doing the job in a sensible fashion. Once again his extravagance and his little learning were dangerous. Needing a more ferocious specter than North Vietnam alone to explain our wading deeper into the quagmire, by 1967 he began talking of "Asian Communism with its headquarters in Peking," which prompted experts on campuses across the nation to rebut with impatient distaste that Asian Communism, following the accidental trend of Communism around the world, had long ago splintered into as many nationalism-Com-

munisms as there are nations to host the ideology, and that
even within China itself Communism has a different shading
from province to province.

From Hongkong, Stanley Karnow, the Washington *Post's*
highly regarded correspondent on Far Eastern affairs, wrote:
"The Administration's present effort to portray Communist
China as an aggressive, expansionist power poised to sweep
across Asia is widely considered by the community of Far East
experts here to be inaccurate, misleading and, perhaps most
important, potentially detrimental to future United States
policies in the Orient. As analysts here see it, China is scarcely
the menacing colossus described by Vice President Humphrey
. . . but rather a poor, backward country primarily focused
on its own critical domestic problems and desperately seeking
strategists to hasten its lagging development." But Humphrey
could not afford to share this tolerance; to have done so would
have destroyed the sen-sen-scented smoke, the Yellow veil of
terror his imagination and rhetoric had flung over the Asian
continent—an atmosphere quite necessary to make his dedica-
tion to the Johnson program seem even remotely logical. He
was driven to wilder and wilder hyperbole. After the diplomatic meeting in Hawaii in 1966, where President Johnson
embraced Premier Ky of South Vietnam and proclaimed the
"Declaration of Honolulu," Humphrey called the outcome of
that hasty and misshapen conference a "Johnson Doctrine for
Asia" and likened it to the Monroe Doctrine in the Western
Hemisphere. He said, "If that meeting is studied carefully, I
think it has as much significance for the future of Asia as the
Atlantic Charter had for the future of Europe." And when this
was received with hoots and roars of bitter laughter from editorial writers and Asian scholars everywhere, Humphrey re-
torted in anger, "This was one of the most important meetings
of modern times, a blueprint of hope. It grieves me when people
make a mockery of the Declaration of Honolulu or of the
meeting there." Such blunders, however, have not silenced
him.

Despite his concern for disarmament and humanitarian aid,

Humphrey on balance emerges as a war liberal advocating what A. A. Ekirch described as "a militant, interventionist nationalism, masquerading as idealistic internationalism."

Humphrey, of course, never joined the tiny band of Senate liberals with nerve enough to actually vote against the more extreme Cold War aberrations; yet on rare occasions he has spoken out against militarism. In 1959, when it looked as if the United States might have to fight Communist China to save that kept American pussycat Chiang Kai-shek, Humphrey attacked the Formosa Resolution's ambiguity concerning the U.S. obligation to defend the Chiang-held islands just off the Chinese mainland. But Humphrey ended up voting for the resolution which passed 85-3 (Morse of Oregon, Langer of North Dakota, and Lehman of New York dissenting). In 1959 Humphrey joined Senators Fulbright and Kennedy to criticize the military emphasis of the foreign-aid program. They persuaded the Senate to increase the authorization for the Development Loan Fund. But even such mild dissents by Humphrey were extremely uncommon.

"The world annually spends more than $120 billion on industries related to war and destruction—a figure greater than the total annual income of the poorer half of the world," the ghost of Humphrey observed in *The Cause Is Mankind*, his 1964 campaign book. "This is a shocking waste of resources, even more so since none of the smaller countries can buy, with the military dollar, more than passing security against another small neighbor. And no one can buy security against large-scale aggression in this nuclear age." In a 1959 speech at Yale University, Humphrey said: "Disarmament should be the core of American foreign policy. We are a nation dedicated to peace and we know that peace is always threatened by an arms race. A case can be built for an armament structure as a holding action, but a world armed to the teeth is a dangerous world. . . ."

Despite such sentiments Humphrey remains a strong advocate of American salvation through increased military spending. He is not uneasy as the No. 2 man in the Administration that in 1968 sought $79.8 billion for the military—second in history only to the $81.2 billion in 1945 at the end of World War II. Humphrey's voting record goes far beyond the concept of arming "as a holding action," which he suggested in his Yale speech.

"Free government cannot stand unless it is prepared to defeat aggression without or within," is the more authentic HHH voice heard in *The Cause Is Mankind*. "Liberalism becomes a mockery when it is spineless and cowardly. No slogans, no long-range policies offering economic and social progress, can defeat the threat of immediate, naked force. . . . Only force itself—and the willingness to use it swiftly, powerfully, and courageously—can maintain a free government in power when subversion and terrorism are used against it." It does not seem to bother him that this view begs the question of whose force—that of the United States or of the government threatened by revolution?

Some of Humphrey's friends find his new role of apologist for everything Johnsonian rather repulsive. War-created inflation? Nonsense, he told the Business Council in the fall of 1965. At the slightest sign of inflation, "President Johnson would take appropriate fiscal and financial action, I can assure you." (Two years later, with only a runaway interest rate holding back runaway inflation, Johnson began to tentatively consider a tax rise.) Straight-faced, on Dec. 7, 1965, HHH said, "As of today there is no immediate threat of inflation." The very next day Federal Reserve Board chairman William McChesney Martin raised interest rates as an emergency restraint. When the choice is between loyalty and honesty, Humphrey is not hard put to choose. A couple of months earlier Humphrey had been asked if the Administration contemplated an embargo on travel abroad, the kind that today, in 1968, it is considering, and Humphrey denied it hotly. "The

position of the Administration," he said, "is never negative."
At every opportunity he has argued that LBJ's emphasis on
"creative consensus" is "bold and beneficial." He works up a
good peeve whenever an ex-insider reveals some of the knife
play in the executive department. When, in 1965, Arthur
Schlesinger, Jr., reported that John Kennedy wanted to dump
Rusk, Humphrey was grieved by the disclosure. "I don't think
it helps a great deal to be talking out of school. In government if we can't talk frankly to one another without having
somebody report it the next day, no one is going to say anything." He seemed to miss the point that Schlesinger wasn't
talking about something "the next day" after it happened; he
was reporting on something that had happened two years
previously. Although in the old days Humphrey, as much as
anyone on the Foreign Relations Committee, had enjoyed
baiting Secretary of State Dulles in his personal appearances
before that group, Humphrey defended Rusk's many refusals
to appear before the committee. Although in 1956 Humphrey
said he would never agree to exempt the Israel-Arab dispute
from the 1956 campaign discussion, as proposed by Dulles,
in 1968 he is urging candidates to treat the Vietnam War in
a neutral bipartisan fashion.

But of course nowhere does Humphrey so excel at carrying
the message of Lyndon Johnson as on that most sensitive
front, the war. "In Vietnam," Humphrey told a group of University of Pittsburgh students, "only the Viet Cong has committed atrocities." With the beginning of the permanent
bombing of North Vietnam, Humphrey escalated our com-
mitments as well. Previously he had said that American troops
were in Vietnam to defend the freedom of the Southern non-
Communists, but on February 9, 1965, he changed this to,
"We're not only fighting to protect the freedom of Vietnam
but of all Southeast Asia." As criticism of the war began to
mount in the summer of 1965, Humphrey showed his sensi-
tivity by toning down reports from the front. In a speech
delivered in Minneapolis in July of that year he changed a
phrase which originally said the war would touch "hundreds

of thousands of American families" to make it read merely "thousands" of families, and he struck from the speech altogether the sentence that conceded that the war could mean "the expenditure of great resources—of money, material, and, yes, of human life." In place of this he stuck in a sentence saying that the war did not mean a choice between war and domestic projects, that both could be supported. (This particular bit of conmanship is too much even for loyal Hubert, and by 1967, in a speech to members of Plans for Progress, he was admitting, "There is no question that Vietnam, and our other international obligations, do require resources which might otherwise be devoted to building wider and better opportunity in America." But this is, naturally, a theme he does not like to return to.)

Beginning in 1965, Humphrey began to bear Johnson's personal cross. "It just breaks my heart to see the liberal community—no, some of the liberal community—act the way they do," he lamented in an interview with Julius Duscha of the Washington *Post*. And in the same year, talking with Emmet John Hughes of *Newsweek*, he offered an incredible defense of the master: "He [LBJ] is ringed by myths that hurt. Let me dispel three. He is supposed to be a tyrant of opinion. The truth is that he *insists* on dissent. If he smells a doubt in you, he will *force* it out. If he has a seemingly airtight case, he will command a brief to be drawn on the other side. He is said to be a bit of a hard-fisted militarist. He is nothing of the sort. I've seen him with some of his generals and their more militant plans for Southeast Asia. He will listen respectfully. And then he may go right down the line of them: 'No, General. . . . No, General. . . . No . . . . No.'"

Although an enthusiastic warrior, fickleness comes first with Humphrey. Briefly, a few years ago, he was saying things like this: "In the Far East, our military-oriented program should be gradually scaled down, just as our direct involvement in Southeast Asia should be gradually curtailed." The following year, biographer Griffith (who worked on Humphrey's Senate staff for four years), revealed: "In the periodic

flareups of crisis in Southeast Asia he [Humphrey] sees first
not a set of military or diplomatic puzzles, but rather a basic
political problem. He has grown impatient at White House
meetings as he has heard one man after another focus almost
all attention on the military aspects of U.S. involvement in
Laos or Vietnam and has sought to bring more attention to
what he sees as a neglected need—governments in Southeast
Asia which are responsive to the needs and wants of the
people, and thus people who are loyal to the governments."

If Humphrey offered such advice to Johnson, the President
obviously ignored it.

"I have my own views," Humphrey told the Associated
Press in 1966. "I have my own conscience. I wear no man's
collar. President Johnson's foreign policy is one I've been
involved in as one of his advisers. When I disagreed, I expressed my differences. He accepted some of them." Humphrey's conscience seldom has interfered with his enthusiasm
for the Vietnam War. In 1967, he suggested in a radio interview that the war might be ended by bringing non-Communist members of the National Liberation Front, political arm
of the Viet Cong guerrillas, into some future South Vietnamese government. That resembled a 1966 statement made
by Senator Robert Kennedy which Humphrey denounced because it was like "putting a fox in the chicken coop." The
Johnson Administration, however, quickly disassociated itself
from Humphrey's proposal and he obediently changed his
position again.

Despite such slips, the score card LBJ keeps on his vice
president must rate him very high. Humphrey has even
learned to sound like he is saying exactly the same thing as
Johnson, without using the exact words. While Johnson prefers to damn the "cussers and the doubters," Humphrey uses
the expression "whiners and quitters." One of Johnson's favorite sayings is, "Don't spit in the soup; we've all got to eat."
Humphrey changes that only to: "You don't put poison in the
soup you're going to have to eat." One of Johnson's bitter
amusements over the past couple of years has been to pull

from his pocket, and read to any visitor, clippings from some of the anti-Vietnam war columnists he hates the most, old clippings of their columns in which they advised against going into World War II. Humphrey joined the game. Speaking to a luncheon of the AFL-CIO's political action group in Washington in October, 1967, he ridiculed "these weekend wonders" (columnists and commentators) who urged the U.S. "to shrink its forces three months before Pearl Harbor and said we should make peace with Hitler after his forces had rolled across the lowlands." (He mentioned no names and read from no clippings.) But in nothing was he so adroit in supporting Johnson's position as in his defense, direct and oblique, of the rulers of South Vietnam at a time when the press was generally inclined to denounce them as talented crooks. Oh, sure, President Thieu and Vice President Ky might not be running exactly an honest administration, but shucks, said Humphrey, "some American cities could teach the South Vietnamese some lessons in how to operate a corrupt government." Why throw stones at such Americanized mischief? "We might spend a little time cleaning our own stables before we start lecturing, piously lecturing, other people." Certainly *he* wasn't going to lecture the South Vietnamese, and so when he arrived in that country in the fall of 1967, according to the Washington *Post,* "Humphrey did not attempt to put any pressure on Thieu or Ky to accelerate reforms."

(Humphrey's mimickry of Johnson finally led some to suspect the sincerity of everything he said. Writing in November, 1967, Alan Otten, Washington bureau chief of the *Wall Street Journal,* commented: "On a recent West Coast trip he met and effusively praised longshoreman-philosopher Eric Hofer; many thought his warmth was due less to their own conversation than to the fact that Mr. Hofer had lauded Lyndon Johnson and been embraced at the White House a few days earlier.")

Humphrey clearly has tied his political future to an American victory in the Vietnam War, which he acknowledged in a remark on a trip to Malaysia in 1967. The future of mankind may hang on the outcome of the Vietnam War, he said, adding: "If it's a colossal failure, I know what happens to me." Too much shouldn't be made of the slim contradictions in Humphrey's statements on the Vietnam involvement over the years. ". . . I support our policy in Southeast Asia and Vietnam—I support it now as I have over the past twelve years," he said in a 1967 speech.

It has become his job, the most difficult task in the nation today, to go over the country describing Johnson as a peacemaker and the military policy of the Administration to be a "passion for peace" (two months after he became vice president, in a radio show with Senator Clark, he admitted the Vietnamese situation "doesn't lend itself much to talk of peace," but he has since carefully avoided a repetition of that candor). He has become, in Mary McGrory's words, the cheerful cheerleader of the war.

At times his enthusiasm has bordered on the obscene. "This is our great adventure and a wonderful one it is," he told staff members of the American Embassy in Saigon in 1967. Humphrey also expressed grotesque excitement about the war in a 1966 interview on CBS-TV when he said Vietnam is "almost like the first voyage of an explorer into a new land. The ship has almost been storm-tossed on the shore, but we are there. We are going to be in Asia for a long, long time."

His Vietnam commercials, if hard to accept, are at least varied. Humphrey has argued that the Johnson Administration has dispatched 500,000 troops to South Vietnam and is spending an estimated $30 billion a year there for these reasons: to prevent World War III, to contain the Communist Chinese, to protect "our own national security," to stop Communist subversion and aggression in Asia, to protect freedom and self-determination, to help make South Vietnam more prosperous, to bring the Great Society to Asia, to honor our commitments.

In a speech to his home-state Democratic leaders in Minnesota, Humphrey turned theologian and interpreted the Bible's admonition, "Blessed are the peacemakers," to mean an endorsement of the Johnson Administration's war policy in Viet-

nam. "Not the walkers, nor the talkers, but the peacemakers,"
Humphrey said, although the American Friends Service Committee pointed out that the U.S. Government by 1966 had
rejected at least seven tentative peace feelers from North
Vietnam. "No nation," he said on another occasion, "wants
peace more than ours." Once again he seemed to be sharing
the neo-fundamentalist sentiments and values of his idol Wilson, who preached, "I will not cry 'peace' as long as there is
sin and wrong in the world." And Humphrey echoed, late in
'67, "I have not forgotten the lessons of the thirties, when men
cried 'peace,' and failed a generation."

His loyalty has been physical as well. At a time when the
President, because of the threatening attitude among many
citizens, cannot go into the major cities and expose himself—
but instead sticks to military bases and NASA and defense
facilities for his "public" appearances—Humphrey has stout-
heartedly gone into the midst of the rabble.

And he has not always come through without some rough
stuff and the threat of more. At Stanford University in 1967,
when he addressed the student body on the peacefulness of
the Johnson administration, and gave them the assurance that
soon Hanoi would realize "the ball game is over," his sanguine
clichés became too much for the crowd to bear and 2,000 students and faculty members gathered at the rear exit to hoot
and jeer him when he emerged. Humphrey, going to a win-
dow to see if the coast was clear, was greeted with angry
shouts of "Shame! Shame!" He slipped out a side entrance and
hurried to his car, pursued by students shouting "Shame!"
Humphrey was enraged, told reporters for his favorite magazine, *U.S. News & World Report*, that the students were
"hooligans—just a group of ruffians. They threw urine which
they had saved up on the police." *Commonweal* magazine
said no throwing of urine was observed by anybody but
Humphrey and *U.S. News*. It was perhaps rougher than Humphrey's normal engagement with the youth of the nation, but
apparently symptomatic of the way they view him.

Abroad Humphrey had found that representing the foreign

policy and the military policy of his leader is even more demanding. On his trip to Europe in 1967 he was the target for some poorly aimed rotten eggs, fruit, and firecrackers in Brussels; in Germany eleven students were arrested for plotting to assassinate him. (Later they were released.) He was splattered with yellow paint in Rome. In Florence, they tried to hit him with eggs.

Shaking its middle-aged gray head admiringly, the Washington *Post* editorialized in January, 1968, "Give Hubert Humphrey credit for courage. No sooner does Congress make a savage slash in American aid to Africa than he heads off on a diplomatic safari to show Africa that the United States cares." In Ethiopia he passed up the opportunity to speak to students at the Haile Selassie University who, while he visited elsewhere, burned an effigy of President Johnson; he cut short his stay in Mogadishu, Somalia, out of fear of violent demonstrations. (Typically, he took with him as an adviser on this African trip one Irving Brown, a big man in the Meany-Lovestone union spook corps, who in an earlier era made quite a name for himself dispensing CIA funds in Europe to crush the radical labor movement.)

From both tours, Humphrey returned claiming victories.

Now and then he has fought back. Of the foreign detractors visible on the International Days of Protest, he said: "Do you think those demonstrations were organized by some fine little social club? They were organized by an international apparatus. Ninety-five percent of the demonstrators are no more Communists than you or I. But the international Communist movement organized it [the protest] and masterminded it."

By Appointment
to The King

To compensate for the taunts he was getting from some of his old allies in the Americans for Democratic Action, Humphrey persuaded Johnson to add John Roche to the White House staff as a kind of jester in residence, a professional counter-taunter, and he has been good at the job. Roche, a former national chairman of the ADA and a former dean at Brandeis, was the first to quit the ADA in 1968 when it endorsed the presidential candidacy of Senator Eugene McCarthy; as he left, Roche remarked that he expected McCarthy [a Catholic] "on his trip to Disneyland" to wind up in a monastery sooner than he would wind up in the White House. Humphrey's strategy had, at one level, paid off with slugs.

When word got back to Humphrey that some of his old buddies were calling his patter "slavish" and reminiscent of Richard Nixon, he grew red, started to say one thing, stopped, and finally dismissed their protest as "the knee-jerk liberal line." He sat for a few moments silently in his chair, staring at his desk, then swiveled slowly to look at the seal of the Vice President on his wall, the eagle's wings down, its claws holding only one arrow. "Some say I have changed." He paused. "I have."

And he has, but not in the way most of his unhappy liberal

friends think. They think he has drowned his true feelings out of loyalty to the office. "Hubert faces the realities of power which are quite different from what he faced when he was not in power," says former Senator Paul Douglas, thinking of economic affairs, not the war, for he is a hawk himself. "Hubert's heart is still good." Joseph Rauh, thinking only of the war, said, "I'll tell you about Hubert. When I decided to go for McCarthy I went and told him I was going to work for McCarthy, and he didn't try to dissuade me. What he did, however, was to make a firm talk on why the war was right, and he believes in the war. And when he finished, I said, I know you believe in the war, and I wouldn't question your sincerity but I believe if you were president you'd have us out of Vietnam in ninety days. He said, 'I just told you I agree with everything the President has done.' I said, 'I think you *think* that and I believe you honestly *believe* that, but you don't have the kind of independent judgment about that you would have if you were president and unrestricted by the views of anybody else.' He denied it. He says he agrees with Johnson 100 percent. All I'm saying is that I believe if Hubert were president, his visceral liberalism, which I believe is there, would get us out of the war." Rauh just wouldn't take yes for an answer. There are countless Humphreyites like that all over Washington, all over the country. For an even better illustration of this, another conversation with Senator Clark:

Q. Have you talked to him since he's become vice president? On what issues does he sound like the old Hubert?

CLARK: Yes, I've talked with him quite a bit. He gives me the impression that he's in there slugging just as hard as he can for sweetness and light, "all those things we've always longed for . . . gee, it's nice to see you lookin' swell, baby." And that he's the *one* force that holds off much worse in foreign affairs.

Q. The *one* force?

CLARK: He and Goldberg.

Q. But he is happy about our being there, isn't he?

CLARK: He says he is. Doesn't he have to say so? Isn't he a trained seal?

Q. You're the one to say. You're his friend.

CLARK: Well, I know I'm a friend. *I* wouldn't have done it —I would have quit. Wouldn't have run.

Q. But the point is, if he's a fellow who can adapt, and he obviously can, is he incapable of playing honest with you, of saying, "Joe, you know I don't like to be over there but what the hell, I'm a vice president now and I've got to be an alter ego. I can't speak what is in my heart until I'm president or out of this office"?

CLARK: He can imply it and he *has.* But it would be disloyal for him to say that to me when he knows how I feel about Johnson.

Q. But he has implied it?

CLARK: Yes. [Goes into an imitation] "Jesus, Joe, if you knew what I had to put up with. I'm in there every day. . . ."

Q. Meaning, pitching for your side?

CLARK: Yeah.

Q. So you have given your argument to him, time and again?

CLARK: Yes. "Goddammit, Hubert, why do you do this? You don't have to do this. You know it's not right." . . . [Switches again to an imitation of Humphrey] "I just think I have to fight from inside. I can't come out in the newspapers. I'm representing your point of view in there every day and getting my head just as bloody as it can be. Don't think I'm not in there slugging because I am."

Q. Well, if he has a bloody head, is that why he cries so much?

CLARK: He is being torn up. In pieces. God, he's Hamlet. Stevenson was very much the same. Except Adlai was more remote. I think Hubert is being torn to pieces.

The conclusions drawn by these close friends are, so far as one can discover by combing Humphrey's career for telltale tendencies, pure wishing. They are a pathetic "Say it ain't so, Hubie." But it is so. Humphrey has not changed. And he is not cloaking his true feelings. When Humphrey says he has changed, he means, surely, that he no longer *has* to disguise his true feelings. He has changed to a new honesty: he no longer must pretend to be the smashing young liberal who will give the Minneapolis Red-infiltrated unions a fair shake, no longer must he pretend to be the liberal who will purify the DFL for the All-American leftists, no longer pretend to be the leader of the liberal bloc who can deal with the leadership successfully. Now he *is* in the leadership, and he can say straight out, as he did a few months ago, "I suppose I'm left of center. I wouldn't deny that. But very moderately left of center." Now he openly jeers at the "tired radicals, the militants of the 1930's who are the absentees of the 1960's"—the absentees he helped destroy. Quite accurately *Fortune* magazine appraised him in 1965: "After allowance for differences between Minnesota and Texas, there is not much gap between his liberalism and Johnson's."

There is no reason to doubt Humphrey's word, and every reason to take his word, when he says, "Nor should some of my old friends imagine that I support some basic Administration policies merely because of constricting official involvement. I am supporting them out of clear intellectual commitment."

This is true not only in regard to the Johnson war policy but also in regard to the Johnson favoritism for big business.

To maintain his credentials as the "prairie populist" in the 1950's, he frequently berated the Eisenhower Administration for knuckling under to big business. In 1950, speaking in Richmond, Virginia, he said "growing monopoly" was the greatest danger facing America. In 1952, he called the Tidelands oil bill "the greatest steal in the history of this generation." In 1953 he said big business is "calling the tune" for the Eisenhower administration on labor as well as "every other issue" and he was still on that theme on that May morning in 1956 when, with handsome theatrics, flailing his arms and shouting, the Young Democratic Club cheering him on, Humphrey made Washington's old Willard Hotel shiver to its conservative foundation. "Eisenhower's Administration is not motivated by the crusading spirit," he cried. "It is for big business and of big business. Last year was the billion dollar year—General Motors made a billion dollars and the farmers lost a billion dollars. The big business concept of government has gone so far it would be a miracle if you could find a farmer in the Department of Agriculture."

This kind of talk, spread over the years, gave many business men around the country the wrong idea. They did not have the advantage of their several colleagues in Minneapolis who had quietly eased Humphrey to the top. The ol' boys of Minneapolis are still chuckling about the trick they pulled in 1945 when the Minneapolis Junior Chamber of Commerce voted Humphrey the city's "outstanding young man" of the year. It was part of big business's big buildup. The decision had been secretly arranged by what Bradley L. Morison, editorial writer for the Minneapolis *Times* later called, enjoying the deception, "a prime array of bank presidents, industrial leaders, and senior executives of almost unimpeachable Republican standing."

But the wealthy Old Guard of Minneapolis had been so stealthy about their part in the Humphrey buildup and he had been so successful in hamming himself up as a liberal that in 1964, when Johnson decided to make Humphrey his running mate, some re-imaging had to be done. Part of the job was turned over to Johnson's long-time intimate friend, the oil-rich Texas Republican Robert B. Anderson, who had been Ike's Secretary of the Treasury and Secretary of the Navy. Anderson introduced Humphrey into the right circles. Another of the important shapers was Herman Nolen, board chairman of McKesson & Robbins, the drug firm. (In May, 1968, when Dr. James L. Goddard, the reform-minded head of the Food and Drug Administration, announced his resignation, it was noted by the Washington Post that Goddard had been under intensive fire from the drug industry and from drug retailers, and therefore had "aroused the anger . . . of Vice President Humphrey." Apparently he was already paying off his debts.) Humphrey took it up from there, speaking to groups of elite businessmen at every opportunity, presenting his "new" self. Suddenly the word was out, and it was understandably received as rather startling news. Austin C. Wehrwein, writing in *The New York Times*, saw, with surprise, Humphrey "emerging as an advocate of a new kind of 'tactical moderation' as a substitute for 'fiery debate by professional liberals.' The Democrat whom liberals have always regarded as 'reliable, available Hubert,' as he has put it, has become a champion of business-government partnership, even a defender of bigness in business."

But back home in Minneapolis it was a joke.

Frank Premack, Minneapolis *Tribune* writer, observed:

"It has become fashionable these days to think that Hubert Horatio Humphrey's wooing of the nation's corporations represents a switch in his tactics and a mellowing of his political views. As the story goes, the Humphrey of Old, who was Democratic–Farmer-Labor mayor of Minneapolis and then Senator from Minnesota, was a flaming prolabor liberal who neither wanted nor needed business backing; while Hubert Humphrey, now Vice-President, has adopted economic principles considered more fitting to middle age and has turned his back on the table of labor to dine with big business. . . .

"The story of the Great Change tickles the business and labor leaders of this state who knew Hubert Humphrey back when. The story, they say, is myth."

And thereafter Premack disturbed some old buried bones to prove his point, and threw in a quote from Mayor Naftalin, "He never assailed the economic royalist. His reputation as a flaming liberal was based on civil-rights and labor legislation—he was never a doctrinaire liberal. . . ."

Far from being offended by Premack's disclosures, Humphrey went out of his way to call the *Tribune's* piece to the attention of the *U.S. News* in an open letter. ("I think it helps give some balance and perspective on my more recent utterances and actions relating to the American economy.") And in the same letter to *U.S. News*, which would of course go into the hands of the more conservative people around the country, Humphrey ticked off other signs of his high regard for big business: "I strongly supported the investment tax credit when many others were opposed to it. . . . I strongly supported the proposal to establish a Communications Satellite Corporation. I did this in the face of bitter opposition from some of my friends in ADA and the liberal wing of the Democratic Party. . . . I was an early advocate of a reduction in both corporate and personal income taxes. . . . I led the fight in my own state to amend the state constitution to provide a more favorable tax climate for the iron-ore and steel industry."

In measuring the tip of the Humphrey scales between labor and management, one cannot go by what he says: he has said so many flattering and so few critical things about both sides. The best measure is, which side has he struck at when it displeased him? And the answer is labor. One does not have to go back to his betrayal of local labor in the choice of a police chief for Minneapolis. One can come up to the late 1950's when Humphrey voted for the Landrum-Griffin labor reform bill, an act of heresy in the eyes of most liberals and all laborites, and one which he hardly succeeded in excusing with his statement, "You don't legislate in a vacuum. I was convinced that if we did not pass that labor bill we would have got a worse one next year." The vote itself, however, is not so illuminating as his reaction to labor's criticism of it. Humphrey can be quite spiteful, and this was one of those occasions. When he heard the criticism that was being leveled at him by officials of the Central Labor Union in Minneapolis, he got George Meany, president of the AFL-CIO, to investigate the CLU to see if it was conducting its affairs properly. Apparently Humphrey had been tipped off to what was going on. The CLU's operational funds were low, so it had borrowed some from the pension fund; this was irregular, perhaps, but it was exactly what the national AFL-CIO was doing with its pension fund. Meany, at Humphrey's

behest, put the CLU under a trusteeship, sent out a strong-
man who antagonized half the union officials in Minneapolis,
and succeeded in splitting the CLU. It is still split, and the
laboring movement in the state is to that extent much weaker.
Humphrey has never pulled that kind of thing on management.

Nowadays when he is unhappy with management he subjects it to no more than the kind of scolding it might receive
from a spokesman for Moral Re-Armament. To one group of
businessmen meeting in Washington not long ago he said,
"I'm not telling you what to do, but you go up to the Metropolitan Club and spend more on drinks in an hour than it
takes to send a kid to camp for two weeks." And his idea of
toughness was conveyed to another business group when he
said, "If it's a choice between an extra one percent of profit
for you or an education for somebody else, I'm going to be
for the education."

Some have unreasonably suggested that Humphrey could
at least show the good taste of keeping his mouth shut when
confronting the imponderables of the war. Early in 1966, after
a briefing by Humphrey, who had just returned from the Far
East, Senator Wayne Morse said he had talked tougher than
McNamara or Rusk, adding "I think he has lost all his per-
suasiveness among people who think." On a February 11,
1968, "Meet the Press" show, Charles Murphy of NBC asked
Senator Eugene McCarthy, "Let's say your roles were reversed.
Suppose you were chosen vice president. What would you be
doing, would you be defending the President's war policies
as Mr. Humphrey is?" McCarthy answered: "I don't think I
would be. I have said this before. I think the role of the vice
president really depends upon the individual's conception of
it. At least, I think, when one disagrees with the President
on a policy of this kind, you can be quiet as a vice president.
I don't think there is any way in which a vice president can
be compelled to support publicly a position taken by a president with which he disagrees. And I anticipate that if I were
the vice president now, I think I would be quiet."

(McCarthy and Humphrey have been close acquaintances, but not bosom buddies. McCarthy has never forgiven Humphrey for standing aloof when he, McCarthy, was fighting for the DFL convention nomination to the Senate in 1958. Furthermore, while Humphrey was acting neutral, Humphrey people openly worked for McCarthy's rival, Eugenie Anderson. Still, the two men have a kind of middleclass honkie compatibility.)

Such comments as McCarthy's, that of a political colleague, are obviously intended to put Humphrey on the spot by suggesting that if he doesn't believe what he says about the war, he needn't say it. But the answer to that is that there is nothing wrong with Humphrey's talking all he wants to in defense of the war since he does believe in it.

If no other act of Humphrey's has proved that, his effort (sincere or not) to dissuade Johnson from stepping down stamped indelibly his approval on the war. The one best chance to end the war would be by ridding the presidency of Johnson; this was generally accepted; and yet, when Johnson went by Humphrey's apartment on the morning of March 31, the day he was to announce his withdrawal from politics as of the end of this term, Humphrey actually tried to block this most hopeful act. By his own account, "I tried to talk him out of it." If he actually wanted Johnson to stay on, then he wanted the war to continue; there is no other interpretation. But in addition to that, it would be absurd to expect him to keep quiet for other reasons. First of all, he is physiologically incapable of silence. Secondly, Humphrey knows very well that he would never receive the endorsement of the Johnson forces if he showed the slightest gnawing of doubt in regard to the war. And he has always been guided by ambition, with ethics struggling to keep up. And thirdly, Humphrey is grateful to Johnson for making him what he is today. Back in the early 1950's, Johnson said of Humphrey, "I wish I could be that boy's trainer." In the last three years he has had the opportunity as never before, and Humphrey has responded in a way that must give Johnson satisfaction.

"I am vice president because he made me vice president," said Humphrey, speaking as a happily plastic Pygmalion. And on another occasion, "Every word we utter, everything we do, reflects directly on the President and on the White House. We must dress, act, and speak with dignity, wisely and prudently—and with that in mind. The first duty of the vice president is loyalty. I must be his devoted and loyal friend and support." He *likes* Johnson; he *likes* the Johnson style, once comparing it with deep satisfaction to the Kennedy Administration in this way: "It's like the difference between the court of Louis XIV and the early American Republic under Andrew Jackson." He left no doubt as to which he preferred. As for Johnson's basic conservatism, Humphrey has never seen it that way, or at least he has never seen Johnson as basically more conservative than he himself is. When he and Johnson first went to the Senate in 1949, Humphrey introduced him to his wife as "that new liberal Democratic Senator from Texas." Others in those days—an era when Johnson sneered at "all those bleeding heart liberals, those red-hots, red-eyes, and pinkos"—would have considered this to be a social gaff, but Humphrey has always felt that Johnson was more liberal than generally rated, just as he has felt himself to be more conservative than generally rated. "The President and I have known each other a long, long time," he said recently. "I fully knew the difficulties and opportunities of such work with him. I went in with my eyes open. And I have never regretted it."

The loyalty is not entirely one-sided. True, Johnson has shipped Humphrey off to Asia with so little pre-junket tutoring that he made a fool of himself at several stops. John Randolph of the Los Angeles *Times* reported this Humphrey happening at a 1967 diplomatic gathering in Saigon: "Going up to the Laotian delegate, Prince Outhong Souvannavong, chairman of the Laotian Royal Council, Humphrey inquired enthusiastically: 'And how is your wonderful President?' The Prince was momentarily taken aback, hesitated and then replied, 'But Mr. Humphrey, we still have our king you know.' A moment later Humphrey said almost the same thing to the Thai delegate—who similarly was compelled to point out that Thailand, too, was still a monarchy. Unabashed, Humphrey tried it again with Foreign Minister Narcisco Ramos of the Republic of the Philippines—and finally hit the jackpot."

On occasion Johnson has made sport of Humphrey's dignity by hoisting him onto a horse and equipping him with a totally unsuitable cowboy hat, down on the ranch. He has treated him to the indelicacies that any servant of Johnson must contend with. But on the other hand, the rushed assignment to Asia at the end of 1965 was itself an attempt on Johnson's part to bolster the sagging public popularity of Humphrey, as shown by opinion polls. "Operation Help Hubert," Barry Goldwater called it, "the most valiant rescue effort since the evacuation of Dunkirk." Since then Humphrey has been sent back to the Far East to keep his image fresh. And while Johnson subjects Humphrey to indecencies, he will not allow others to do so. "The next time you keep Hubert waiting," he told a White House aide, "I'll kick your ass down the hall."

Johnson has even allowed Humphrey to dissent on one rare occasion though he had to do it slyly. In 1966 Humphrey quietly sided with critics of the Administration's high-interest-rate policy. When Senator Albert Gore was attacking the rates in a Senate speech, he noticed that Humphrey was listening closely and said, "I am so pleased and complimented with the attention of the distinguished presiding officer. I hope he will take this message to the right place." Humphrey sent a response to Gore by page. It read: "The Vice President doesn't set the interest rate. You are making a good fight." Humphrey's hardly concealed unhappiness with the Administration's money policies that year was counted as his first major dissent, and his last.

"The liberal approach must be experimental, the solutions tentative, the test pragmatic," Humphrey wrote in *The American Scholar* in 1955. That *might* be a good description of the liberal approach; but it is one of those reversible descriptions that might also apply to the conservative approach. His statement is, in fact, a perfect specimen of the philosophical genre found in corporations' annual reports. It points in no particular direction; it would as easily be applied to the problems of an expanding tractor dealership as to the problems of birth control. There is, in fact, a predominant tone of commercialism in his advice, and so it is not surprising to hear him, speaking to a U.S. Chamber of Commerce luncheon in May of 1968, take note of the fact that "Some businessmen have even out-liberaled Hubert Humphrey." Why not? To other business groups he has made it plain that this is not hard to do. His liberal standards are such as to make him an authentic American, of a tragic type. Of those who exerted "hero" influences on his early life, William Jennings Bryan (who converted Humphrey's father to the Democratic party) rated very high, not far behind Woodrow Wilson; Humphrey learned some of Bryan's windy speeches by heart when he was young. It will not do to draw too tightly the comparison, but just as the Wilsonian view of the world seems unusually similar to Humphrey's, so does the feeble, wavering decency of Bryan seem strikingly to have its echo in Humphrey's life. R. F. Pettigrew, the great radical U.S. Senator from Humphrey's home state, South Dakota, around the turn of the century, described Bryan as "weak, not corrupt. He is a type of the 'good man' that so often fools the American people. He is vacillating, uncertain, overlooking the fundamental things, ignorant of the forces that are shaping American public life, incapable of thinking in terms of reality, but making phrases as a substitute for thought. He has traveled around the world, yet he knows little of international affairs. He has been from one end of the United States to another, yet he is ignorant of America. This is Bryanism—a fluent tongue, a resonant voice, the plausible statement of half truths, an appeal to the passions and prejudices of the moment, a mediocre mind, and a verbal fealty to 'right,' 'justice,' 'liberty' and 'brotherhood.'" Humphrey has a first-class mind, but in other ways the hero and the hero-worshipper have a remarkable number of characteristics in common.

Happy to be free of some of his old liberal pretentions, Humphrey has not, however, always had the courage to celebrate his freedom in an open, straightforward way. His manner of departure from the Americans for Democratic Action was symptomatic. When the ADA executive committee in February 1968 voted to support Eugene McCarthy for the presidency, everyone wondered what Humphrey would do about his membership in that organization, which he had served as an officer for years and in which many of his oldest friendships were planted. Could he, as Johnson's No. 1 apologist—"our own Vietnam hog-caller," to use Hans Koningsberger's evocative phrase—keep his membership in a group supporting a politician whose main objective was to oppose LBJ's war policies? After the committee meeting ended, several ADA leaders held a press conference at which economist Kenneth Galbraith was asked if he thought Humphrey would resign. "I hope he won't," said Galbraith. "We have a great deal of affection for him." To the same question about Humphrey's quitting Arthur Schlesinger Jr. said, "I don't know. I haven't talked to him about it. But this does put him in a tight spot." As these statements show, the top men in the ADA considered Humphrey still to be a member.

But the next day Humphrey's office announced that, in fact, Humphrey had quit the ADA when he became vice president, three years earlier. "We've not said much about it," commented Norman Sherman, Humphrey's press secretary. Indeed they hadn't. In fact, they hadn't said *any*thing about it. It all sounded slightly phony, and Joseph Rauh, who has always enjoyed serving as Humphrey's Sancho Panza, galloped forward to try to make it all sound a bit more believable.

He insisted that Humphrey had sent a letter of resignation to ADA headquarters, that the letter was supposed to sever all ties with the organization, and that he, Rauh, had in fact helped draft the letter. All of which was camouflage for a timorous, if not sleazily disloyal, performance on Humphrey's part. Actually the letter sent by Humphrey to the ADA on Sept. 2, 1964, did not sever all ties to the organization. Far from it. The letter assures ADA officials that "I shall retain my membership in the organization *at least* through the election. . . ." Until they heard from him to the contrary, the letter clearly implied, he would remain a member. But the ADA never heard from him again. His decisiveness in this, as in so many things, consisted of petering out. Rather than resign forthrightly, he simply ceased paying his dues, tiptoed out the backdoor, and waited for circumstances to force him into announcing that he was gone.

Of course, ADA officials should have suspected that he was up to something. In recent months he had lost few opportunities to belittle the organization that had been so loyal to him. Not long ago he said of the ADA that it "has lost much of its usefulness because most of the positions it formerly held have been enacted into law, thanks to the Democratic Party." This, of course, is true. The ADA, partly because of its bickering leadership and partly because of a vacuous commitment, has become an almost meaningless organization. But some of the ADA's leaders are wise enough to recognize their defects and to seek a rejuvenation. "It cannot be the highest function of the modern liberal," said Galbraith, "to work avidly to accomplish what has already been done." Even in terms of being an effective, spirited influence in debate over the war, the ADA isn't much, as another of its leaders, Congressman Don Edwards, recently admitted: "Speaking candidly, I think that the liberals of our school have not offered effective opposition. The battle ribbons and the scars are worn by the peace organizations, some civil-rights groups and militant students, clergymen, and professors. Our opposition has been polite and civilized, prefaced with protestations of our virtuous anti-Communism and salutations to the good intentions of those in charge of our foreign policy."

But if the ADA is bland, as always, and if it is even more

useless today than it has been in the past, the same defects
can be ascribed to Humphrey, with the added pity that he
does not seem to realize it. The Truman-FDR line that he rode
to the Senate in 1948 is now a cliché, but he is still using it.

But these things are all beside the point at which Humphrey's whole life and career are now focused. He is no longer
interested much in organizational fealties, in issues, in ideologies, in programs, in personal independence, in private judg-
ments, in the tensions of morality, except as these things have
a bearing on his aim to become president. And until recently
that has been altogether a waiting game; to some degree, it
still is. His immediate task, as he sees it, is to stay safe, not
to think up new ideas. The body he serves is still warm, and
still incumbent, and still inhibiting, despite Johnson's promise
to leave the White House, and so he must wait for the national
convention to free him, one way or the other.

There have been moments when he thought he might be
freed earlier. That night late in January 1965, Humphrey was
exhausted. He had worked at his desk in the Executive Office
Building until midnight and had got home around 1 a.m.
The phone rang five times before the call from the White
House awakened him. President Johnson was in the hospital.

"I said nothing to Mrs. Humphrey [he recounted shortly
thereafter]. I went downstairs and just walked around the
house. I went back to the bedroom. Muriel was awake. She
asked if Winston Churchill had passed away. 'No,' I said,
'the President is sick.' We both went downstairs together
and sat and talked."

Here is a conversation that will doubtless never be recorded
but it could brighten any history book with the incandescence
of politics. *Well, Muriel, this is it. This is the break. We
made it. We gambled and won.* If it were said, there would
be nothing insensitive about it. That's what vice presidential
politics is all about, isn't it?

"And then a second call came from the White House, and
I realized my fears and apprehensions were unfounded and
I can now smile again."

And he continued to smile. Smile and wait. That is the role of vice presidents. He once described his office disparagingly as a place in which "you stand around waiting for somebody else to catch cold," and then, perhaps, double pneumonia. Kings in olden days, in a usually futile effort to maintain humility, would often keep near at hand a sign reminding them of their mortality. Vice presidents are the modern equivalent of that sign. Lyndon Johnson might have died; the job of a President is very taxing and his heart had almost stopped forever in the mid-'50s. Or he might have been killed; no politician can make so many enemies as a President and no President had made more than Lyndon Johnson; he had made so many, in fact, that the Secret Service quit announcing the schedule of his travels for fear of an assassination attempt.

The awareness of these possibilities was always there to lift Hubert's spirits if they should sag, which was not likely. And so—when nothing so dramatic as sudden death but merely an ingrained distrust and dislike for Lyndon Johnson (quite measurable by polls) forced him to throw in his hand—the nation discovered, with no surprise at all, that the "girl next door," Hubert the Exuberant, had his enthusiasms all packed and ready. Gee whiz, *certainly* he would run in place of his Chief! Golly yes, he was eager to round up the stragglers and lead the nation on down that long, long trail awinding toward what Hubert ecstatically described, in his announcement speech, as "the politics of Happiness . . . the politics of Joy!" The cities might be ablaze, unemployment in some ghetto retreats might be as much as 40 percent, thousands of Negroes and whites might be literally starving because of an inadequate federal food program, the gold standard might be in precarious condition, the dollar might be anemic—but never mind that right now, because the thing that counted was, he was *running* again, and gosh it felt good. "It's just like a resurrection," he said, adding the only modest statement on record this year, "but much less spectacular."

Already he has gathered around him an imposing force:

most of the big city bosses are with him; the more reactionary
wings of the labor hierarchy have announced for him; Southern Democratic leaders such as Texas Governor John Connally
like him, and say so publicly; and such saints of capitalism as
Henry Ford II, Jacob Blaustein of the American Oil Co., and
financier Sidney Weinberg are not only for him but are helping him to raise a bountiful war chest. On May 1 he spent
three hours in New York and came away with promises for
$750,000. His role in the fund-raising was a 20-minute speech.
That's quite a political honorarium: $37,500 a minute. He has
come a long way from the Huron drugstore.

Big labor, big city bosses, big business, and big boondoggle,
too. As Alan Otten of the Wall Street Journal put it, "There's
the widespread though unproved belief that the Administration's muscle—everything from defense contracts and Model
City grants to patronage and public works projects—is ready
to be applied in the Vice President's behalf."

And if some of the livelier liberals have no heart to follow
this bubbling politician, he will not try to hold them. They
were useful once, but not so useful as others now. He will
see them off amicably, though, for he is that kind of man.
"I'm sure you'll find some of our old friends on the other side
of the fence," he says, waving in a cheerful way at some
imaginary boundary. "They don't have to take orders from
me. I don't take orders from them. Let them make their
choice. I've made mine."

Index